THE
EARLY AMERICAN
HOUSE

THE EARLY AMERICAN HOUSE
By Mary Earle Gould

Household Life in America 1620-1850

With special chapters on the construction and evolution
of old American homes; Fireplaces & Iron Utensils;
Hearthside & Barnyard activities.

CHARLES E. TUTTLE CO., Inc.
Rutland, Vermont

Contents

List of Illustrations

DEDICATION

To my mother

Mrs. John W. Gould

(1855 - 1959)

for her example of courage, steadfastness and determination.

PUBLISHER'S ACKNOWLEDGMENT

The Charles E. Tuttle Co.   wishes to thank
Mr. Francis J. Koppeis,   Innkeeper of The
Wayside Inn, Sudbury, Massachusetts for his
kindness in furnishing the photographs of the
Inn which appear on the endpapers,   the title
page and page 32.

Foreword

WHEN SITTING in conference with the late George Francis Dow in 1934, I had a remark made to me which became a subconscious inspiration and from which this book has materialized. I had met with Mr. Dow and Mr. William Sumner Appleton, of the Preservation of New England Antiquities Society, to confer with them on my research work on wooden ware. Mr. Dow expressed the wish that I do research work on the old kitchens. My answer at the time was to the effect that wooden ware was my hobby, and, with my profession of music, filled my life.

Strangely enough, as I went about my search for wooden ware and early folklore, my interest in the old kitchens and fireplaces besame a vital factor. I took pictures with no apparent need of them, and I left little research material uncovered in regard to fireplaces. My inherent love for early customs and manners stood me in good stead, and I learned much when sitting with persons of the older generations.

Early American Wooden Ware was the result of my hobby in wooden ware. In it is a chapter touching briefly on the old kitchens and fireplace utensils. As a collection of iron utensils began to grow in one of the rooms of my museum, I began to wonder if the chapter on kitchens could not possibly be expanded into a book. Other people soon had the same idea for soon came the request: "Give us now a book on iron ware!" So off I went to explore in earnest old houses for the chimney structure. Some places were private homes and others were museums but I always found a cordial welcome. With flashlight in hand, I went from the dark, damp, cobwebby cellars to the stiffling attics. The chimney structure and the hearth always attracted me with all the signs of everyday life so many years ago. I found much iron ware in unexpected places for my museum and I was amazed at the history I uncovered. I made detailed notes and drawings on the spot in addition to taking many pictures. Soon another book was ready. *The Early American House,* first published in 1948, here is offered in the present revised edition after being out-of-print for many years.

Wood, iron and tin made up our ancestor's equipment and each change meant progress from wooden ware to iron ware to tin ware. I began collecting old tin and learned that the tinsmith had been as important in the community as the wood turner and blacksmith. It was inevitable, I suppose, that I write a book on the subject and *Antique Tin & Tole Ware* published in 1958 completed my trilogy on the household arts in Early American life.

In both my collecting and research work, I have had many loyal friends, seen and unseen. It would be impossible to tell of all my correspondence during these past years, nor of the interest with which my work has been greeted. I learned and profited by contacts with those far more able than I. Perhaps I can express my appreciation to them through the efforts of these books.

Several books have been of assistance in writing several chapters of this particular book. They are books of Alice Morse Earle (of no relation); *The Log Cabin Myth,* by Harold R. Shurtleffe; *Old Houses in New England,* by Knowlton Mixer; *The Story of Architecture in America,* by T. E. Tallmadge; *The Architecture of Colonial America,* by Harold Donaldson Eberlein; *History of American Life,* by Arthur M. Schlesinger; *The Story of Everyday Things,* by Arthur Train, Jr.; Bulletin No. 141, U. S. National Museum; *Iron and Brass Implements of the English and American Home,* by J. Seymour Lindsey; *History of American Manufactures,* by J. L. Bishop; *We Were New England,* by Barrows Mussey; *Every-Day Life in the Massachusetts Bay Colony,* by George Francis Dow; *The House of the Pilgrim Fathers in England and America,* by Martin S. Briggs; and *The Tercentenary of Harvard College,* by Samuel Eliot Morison.

Mary Earle Gould

Worcester, Massachusetts

THE
EARLY AMERICAN
HOUSE

I

Early One-Room Houses and How They Grew

IF IT HAS never been said in poetry or prose, "By their chimneys ye shall know them," then someone has missed the opportunity of describing old American houses. Those chimneys, especially large central chimneys, are a mark of distinction. As one journeys through the old towns, especially in New England, one is impressed with the imposing central chimney — square and rugged it stands astride the roof, boasting of many fireplaces and a base of ample proportions in the cellar. It seems to belong with the small-paned windows, the double-crossed doors and the scraggly lilac hedge keeping guard at one side.

The privations, sickness and suffering, and the wars and strifes that followed the landing of the various groups coming from their mother country have been told countless times, but the research student of early history must search inventories, wills, letters and documents, as well as the few authentic books, to learn of the settling of the new America.

It was in 1605 that John Smith made his first voyage and landed in what is now Virginia, calling it New England. Henry Hudson, in 1609, went up the river that was later to be called by his name, and it was not many years before the English and the Dutch were successful in making settlements. The Pilgrims came over with rosy pictures in their minds of the country where they were to land, pictures based on the accounts of John Smith; a country wonderful for its climate, sea food and natural resources.

In 1631, Pennsylvania was settled by Penn and his followers; not many years later, Swedes settled in Pennsylvania and Delaware. The Dutch and Swedes settled New Jersey, later followed by the English, who also took over New Netherlands from the Dutch, though Dutch influence remained. Thus, in briefest form, is stated the beginning of the early colonies.

The need of shelters was urgent, and the pioneers of New York, Massachusetts and Pennsylvania resorted to a form of cave or dug-out. Some were built in embankments, with three sides of earth, cased with wood, and a fireplace built at the back. Poles were laid across the top and covered with spars or boughs and coarse grasses, and at the front was a door by which to enter. Or the cave house was made by digging a pit in the ground, building a stone fireplace at one end, and lining the sides with timber on which the bark had been left. The floor was of planks and the roof of spars or green sod. The fireplace and chimney structure was of field stones and sticks of wood held by mortar made of clay and grass.

In New England, a still different structure was that called a wigwam, copied not from the American Indian but built after the manner of shelters in England and having a fireplace. In constructing this shelter, small poles stuck into the ground were brought together at the top and fastened, making a dome-shaped roof. A fireplace was built at one side and at the opposite side was a door, which was not a mat such as the Indians used, pushing it aside as they entered, but one of wood swung on withe hinges. At the side of the door, a window covered with birch-bark lining or oiled paper gave little light in that gloomy room. Straw or rushes sufficed for a covering on the floor, and when night came each member of the family rolled himself in skins and slept.

The warm climate of the South did not call for sturdy shelters to give protection from the elements. Awnings of sail cloth, stretched on poles or on four trees gave a covering overhead, and the walls were rails of wood. There was no need of a fireplace for heat. The South also resorted to wigwams covered with skins or bark. One historian says that in 1626 there were thirty houses on Manhattan Island, and all but one of them were of bark.

It has often been stated that log cabins were built by the first settlers, but this has been authoritatively disputed. The Swedes who set-tled in Delaware and New Jersey built log houses, the logs being notched at the ends after the manner of the homes they had left across the water. An occasional log house was put up in New York and Pennsylvania, but it seems certain that log cabins were not the usual first shelters of the early settlers.

Log garrisons were erected in all the villages as a protection against the Indians, but in these the chinks were not filled with clay and mud. As pioneers opened new land more and more to the west, cabins did appear at a later date. But artists have so often portrayed the picturesque cabin of logs as the home of the earliest settlers that present-day generations have accepted it as a truth. An exhaustive study of this matter was made by the late Harold R. Shurt-leffe, whose work was carried on and edited by Samuel Eliot Morison of Harvard College, authorative historian and writer.

Few sawyers or carpenters came over in those first groups of settlers. The men were farm-

BARK WIGWAM, REPRODUCED AT SALEM VILLAGE, MASSACHUSETTS, WAS THE FIRST SHELTER OF THE NEW ENGLAND COLONISTS. *Clayton Jenks.*

(*Right*) REPRODUCTION OF A LOG CABIN INTERIOR BUILT IN ONONDAGA COUNTY, NEW YORK. EXCEPT FOR THE CLOCK, ALL FURNISHINGS BELONG TO THE LATE EIGHTEENTH CENTURY. *L. A. Johnson*

ers or persons of education and accomplishment, and they found it extremely difficult to adapt themselves to hewing out clearings and coping with the elements in such rude surroundings. Frame houses were built as soon as possible, following the temporary dugouts. These houses, rectangular in shape, were built on sills resting on the ground. A fireplace was at one end; there was a door at the side, and a few small windows. An unfinished loft above was reached by a ladder.

Sawing was done in a pit, a custom still carried on in backward countries. One man stood in the pit, which was called a saw pit, and an-other stood on a platform over the pit, on which rested the logs to be sawed. A long saw with two handles was used in a vertical position.

The space between the double walls of the house was filled with broken shale and chopped straw — an operation called nogging, done to keep out the cold. Wide floor boards, made from the huge trees, were laid in two floors, with filling between. Doors were of boards with additional strips nailed crosswise, both for security against the Indians and for protection from the cold blasts of winter. Such doors were called batten doors. Hinges were of wood from blue beech or of willow withes, and latches also were of wood.

OUTSIDE OF AN OLD DOOR SHOW-
ING PANEL DESIGN. DOOR ONCE
OPENED OUT - OF - DOORS, NOW
LEADS TO SHED ADDED AT LATER
DATE. AT BOTTOM IS THE INSIDE
OF THE DOOR. NOTE SMOOTH
SHEATHING WHICH IS ORIGINAL
AND MACHINE-WROUGHT HINGES
WHICH ARE NOT. *Paul W. Savage.*

THE EARLIEST DOORS WERE SOME-
WHAT PRIMITIVE AFFAIRS MADE
OF TWO OR THREE PLANKS HELD
TOGETHER WITH A PAIR OF HORI-
ZONTAL BOARDS (BATTENS)
FASTENED ACROSS THEM ON THE
BACK. HERE IS THE FRONT OF
A BATTEN DOOR FROM THE PAR-
SON CAPEN HOUSE (BUILT
1683) IN TOPSFIELD, MASS-
ACHUSETTS. THE PLAINESS OF
THIS DOOR IS RELIEVED WITH AN
INTERESTING STUD DESIGN.

Generations of today know about a latch string only from the old nursery rhyme, "Cross patch, draw the latch, sit by the fire and spin," or from the saying we sometimes hear, "The latch string is out for you," meaning, "You would be welcome company." The latch string was the only means of opening the door from the outside. It was a cord with a peg tied to the end, which was attached to the latch, thrust through a hole above the latch and hung outside. By pulling the cord, the latch on the inside was lifted and the door could be opened. When anyone wished security, he pulled in the string and the door could not be opened from the outside.

Clapboards and wainscotting were made and used almost at once, for records state that they were being sent to England by 1621. Clapboards originally were called clayboards, because they covered the clay filling between the walls. Panes of glass came from England by 1638. They were diamond-shape and small, which resulted in small windows; the first windows were casement type, swinging out when opened. Sash windows, double hung, came in 1685, and the panes in these, too, were small, but they were rectangular in shape. The early sash windows had different distribution in the lower and upper parts, nine and six, or twelve and nine.

The roofs were built with a long slope, better to shed the rain, and were thatched. This was done over a period of fifty years. In the marshlands by the sea, lots were assigned to each settler for raising grasses or rushes, which were used as thatch for roof covering. Bundles six inches in diameter and varying in length were placed on the roof overlapping each other, and fastened with sticks of willow or hickory.

The part of the chimney above the roof, called the shaft, was built of wood, the sticks laid cob-house fashion, two by two, and the whole daubed with clay. Fire was a constant menace to the thatch, and after many houses had burned down a law was passed that no chimney should be made of wood. Then hand-rived shingles of wood were substituted for the thatch, but these were only a little less likely to catch fire from

BOARDS FOR COLONIAL HOUSES WERE CUT FROM LOGS AT SAW PITS. ONE MAN STOOD BELOW AND ANOTHER ABOVE AND CUT VERTICALLY WITH A LONG TWO-HANDLED SAW. *Gertrude Jekyll.*

the great heat of the chimney. The shingles, when tied in bundles, were called shakes, or shooks. They were rived or split by hand as early as 1640. This was done with a beetle and wedge, and later on a shave-horse. The shingles were from one to three feet in length, and they shed water more readily than did the thatch. In due time, the chimney was built of stones or brick.

Bricks were made from the clay found in the soil by the ocean and in river beds. Jamestown, Virginia, was making bricks by 1611; Massachusetts, in 1629; New Amsterdam, 1628; Maryland, 1652; and Pennsylvania, 1684. The bricks were shipped to many localities, even to great distances, for bricks came to be considered indispensable. Chimneys and fireplaces were made of brick, and in some localities brick houses were built. Sometimes all four sides of brick, or the ends were of brick, with clapboards front and back.

It has been said that the Massachusetts Bay Company of England sent over 10,000 bricks, along with other building materials such as iron, steel, nails, red lead, salt and sail cloth, as necessities. Bricks have been found with the stamp of "London" on them, verifying that bricks were sent from England, although they were not sent in large quantities, or over any great period of time.

Houses were built according to the custom of the country from which the settlers came, each group following to some extent the style of the mother country. Materials were brick, stone and wood. Wood was used predominantly in New England because of the vast forests; field stone and ledge in Pennsylvania and parts of New York state; brick in Maryland, Virginia and the South; stone in the Hudson region among the Dutch and red sandstone in New Jersey — all materials of the local territory. But the various groups also built their homes to some extent according to the nature of the country in which they had settled. In New England, houses, sheds and barns were connected because of the severe weather in winter. In New York state, the Dutch made their homes with the idea of storing, the living quarters occupying the ground floor only, and the upper floors being for storage purposes. A barn was built separately.

In Maryland, Virginia and other parts of the South, the mild climate allowed groups of buildings. It was only a short time before tobacco crops brought much wealth, and it was then that mansions were built for the well-to-do owners. The kitchen was a separate building, and there was a house for the slaves, a stable for the many horses and a coach house for the coaches; in addition, there was a barn, a smoke house, a milk house, a washhouse, a spinning house, a house for preserving meats, built over a running stream, a brew house and a tool house. Some estates had even more buildings, while some had fewer, but each estate, with its varied array of buildings, looked almost like a small village.

The expansion of the one-room house of the early seventeenth century was carried out by adding a second room on the other side of the fireplace, leaving the chimney between, with a small entry in front of the chimney. It was at this period that shingles replaced thatch. Wainscoting was used to make the rooms warmer, even though there was considerable criticism over this innovation.

The floors were made with an under-floor, the space between being filled with a similar filling to that between the two outside walls. Plaster was used as early as the end of the seventeenth century, but not as a general thing. At first it was made of hair from cows' tails and horses' manes, mixed with crushed clam or oyster shells. Later, lime was discovered in the soil in various locations and this was used in making plaster. Rooms were plastered occasionally for the extra warmth thus provided.

Chimneys were built on a stone foundation, sunk into the ground less than a foot. The Jethro Coffin house in Nantucket, built in 1686, has a chimney resting on stone slabs set into the ground, and not until recent years was there any need of re-setting the structure because of sagging.

Cellars are mentioned in records in 1636, but it would be impossible to state when the first excavations were made under a house. They were more often put under a part of the house, to be used as a storeroom, for such space was colder than any other place for storing. Seldom do any of the very old houses have a cellar foundation under the entire structure.

It would appear, therefore, that there was no cellar under the first one-room houses. When additional rooms were built, a cellar was dug,

STEEP THATCHED ROOFS AND WOODEN CHIMNEYS GIVE UNIQUE APPEARANCE TO EARLY COLONIAL COTTAGES REPRODUCED AT SALEM VILLAGE, MASSACHUSETTS. *Clayton Jenks.*

the beams of the house resting on the stone foundations. Thus the research worker can make deductions as to whether the house had only one room in the beginning.

In the first cellars, steps led through the foundation from outdoors, steps of stone that were covered with a wooden bulkhead as a protection. Inside steps came in due time, for convenience, being either stone slabs, wooden logs, or steps made with risers and treads of wood. When various related families shared the home, the cellar was reached by two or sometimes three different flights of steps, according to the division of the rooms above.

An interesting feature of an old house is the nature of the cellar floor, which shows the type of soil in the locality. One old cellar floor is entirely of flat ledges, with very little soil between, and it takes skill to manage one's steps because of the unevenness. The particular section of the country in which this cellar is located is full of ledges of all dimensions, some measuring ten or fifteen feet. The words of the Bible seem to have been taken literally and the house was "built upon a rock."

Another old cellar has a floor of moist clay, which doubtless is common throughout the neighborhood. Such clay was used, too, as a base for the first paint. Peculiarly enough, this old house stands weatherbeaten, with never a coat of paint. In the same neighborhood, in a cellar with a similar clay floor, huge flat rocks were laid along one side of the wall to make a platform for the various barrels of soft soap, cider, apples and the like. Often the platform was raised two or more feet so that the bunghole was elevated and the work of drawing cider or vinegar was made easier. Without doubt, stones made a better cold storage place than did dirt or clay, and one with less dampness.

Cellar foundations were laid with whatever stone was at hand. In one house, the huge boulders are four and five feet in diameter, having been put into place with the help of oxen and two or three men. Other walls show a skillful construction of field stones, the chinks carefully filled with mortar; while some foundations are

of flat stone, loosely set. After two hundred years or more, the foundations, some of them as high as twelve feet, show no signs of sagging or loosening. Much care and time was given to building in those early years, because materials were hard to gather and the tools were primitive.

A trip to one of these early cellars, for wine or cider, stored fruits or vegetables, or for soft soap from the soap barrel, was a precarious one, as is obvious to anyone who undertakes to explore one today. The candle holder had a lip and was hung on a barrel while the necessary article was sought.

The loft of the one-room house was reached by ladder through a hole in the ceiling, and was used as a place for extra beds for children and servants. As the house expanded, the loft gave way to a garret. The word garret seems to be older than the word attic, and is derived from Old English, meaning in its original use a place for refuge or a place for a lookout. Perhaps when the settlers used the space for storage in the seventeenth century, the word attic came to mean the space under the roof; which was a place both for storage and for refuge from the Indians. Bedding, chests, unused implements and furniture, dried herbs, seed corn, the tub of maple sugar which drained from a spigot into a bowl, giving the only known molasses for many years — all of these things found their way into the attic. Memories, too, were there, along with the packages of letters, the papers, clothing and odd trinkets stored in trunks, reminiscent of past days when those brave, hardy ancestors ventured and endured.

With the fear of Indians ever present with the colonists, many houses had a secret stairway built at the side of the chimney, leading to an upper room or to the attic, where there was a means of leaving the house. A secret room has been found in cellars too, with stairs leading to

SPLIT LOGS SET ON TWO RAILS ADEQUATELY SOLVED THE STAIRWAY PROBLEM FOR THE NEW ENGLAND SETTLER. NOTE THE OLD NAILS.

it from the back of the chimney. The Joshua Coffin house (built in 1756) in Nantucket has an inner steep and narrow stairway, with a store-room back of it, running from the cellar to the attic, and terminating in a trap door concealed in the attic floor. There is a secret stairway in the Fairbanks house in Dedham, Massachusetts, and it is thought to have connected with an underground passage through the cornfields.

Perhaps the houses of New England show the development of building more than do those of the other colonies. The expansion from the one-room house to that of two rooms made a small entry with the stairs to the garret against the chimney — and a small entry it was in New England, where icy blasts entered and snow swirled in when the door was opened in the winter. The South had no such need of small entries; there the house had a spacious hall, running the entire length of the house.

FIREPLACE OF THE JOHN ALDEN HOUSE IN DUXBURY, MASSACHUSETTS, SHOWING OVEN IN BACK AND A VARIETY OF HEARTHSIDE UTENSILS IN FRONT. *Clayton Jenks.*

The first stairs were boxed-in — they were, quite literally, stair-cases — and the stairs were steep and narrow, with high risers and narrow treads. Then came stairs that were partly boxed and partly open, with a rail. In houses built at a later period, from studied plans and by artistic designers, there were banisters, balusters and newel posts.

A quotation from *Domestic Life in New England in the 17th Century*, by George Francis Dow, shows that fourteen years after the colonists settled in the new country, comfortable living was general. "The estate of John Dillingham in 1634 comprised two rooms, outbuildings, 30 acres of upland, 60 meadows, (grass land) six acres planting ground near the house of which four were planted with corn. Apple trees and other fruit trees fenced off in a garden. Mare, three cows, two steers, four calves and four pigs." Live stock and fruit trees were brought over as early as 1630, according to other records.

The room at one side of the entry was called the "hall," again a word brought from England; this was the main room, used as kitchen, living room and, in cold weather, bedroom. It was also called the "fire room." The room on the other side of the entry was the parlor, which was the "best room" and company bedroom, occasionally used in more prosperous families as a bedroom for the mistress.

The fireplace in the "hall" or kitchen was large, often measuring eight or ten feet wide, six feet high and six feet deep. High up on the ledges of the chimney rested a lug pole — a heavy pole of wood on which hung the pothooks for the kettles. There was no oven at first, all cooking being done in and over the fire, in iron and brass kettles and pots, with three legs or with none. The iron utensils and those of brass and copper were brought from across the water, until the village blacksmith and the tinsmith produced such utensils, hand-wrought and made to suit the needs of the women folk. Tin ovens, too, were used at an early date. The cooking utensils and methods of cooking are explained in Chapters Two and Three.

A smoke oven was built in the chimney at

(*Left*) Pine cupboard with shelves stacked with china, wooden boxes, and other kitchen necessities. (*Above*) Mugs and pewter plates are right at home in a cupboard of a Salem, Massachusetts, house. *Clayton Jenks.*

one side, and in this were hooks or poles on which hams were hung and smoked. A fire was made of corncobs and hickory bark and the meat smoked for three days, with three successive fires. This, too, is explained more fully in Chapters Two and Three.

Placed by the fire were high-backed settles, a protection from the cold and drafts of the room. The settles were made with boxed seats, in which the bedding was stored. The table on which the family ate was a thick oaken plank set on trestles, and this stood against the wall after each meal, to make more space in that crowded room. (See frontispiece.) For crowded it was, with stools, benches, barrels, buckets, tubs, implements for making butter and cheese, for spinning and weaving and candle making, along with many wooden utensils for cooking and eating.

A large cupboard stood at one side of the fireplace, with open shelves above and doors below, and here the daily utensils and implements were kept. These cupboards were variations of the beautiful oak court cupboards in the mother country, which date back to 1344. In this country, cupboards were made of pine, and many styles appeared, with various names — small cupboard, great cupboard, press cupboard, court cupboard, livery cupboard, hanging cupboard and sideboard. Each had its own use, but they all supplied a place for dishes, board cloths, table cloths and tableware.

A beautiful type of cupboard was the one built into a corner, which appeared about 1710. This had doors below concealing shelves, with narrow shelves above and an arch in the shape of a huge shell. Often this shell was painted blue to resemble the blue of the sky.

Pewter came with the owners to the new land and gave a semblance of the prosperous days in the past. China, too, decorated the shelves when whaling vessels began to sail the high seas, taking various commodities to distant lands and returning with choice articles, such as silk, dishes and ornaments, embroidery, shawls, trays and fans. But for everyday use, it was wooden ware that held full sway, and the supply increased as the demand for it arose.

The dye tub stood on the hearth, for it was only a matter of time before every family dyed its flax and wool and wove and made it into garments and coverings for beds. A spinning wheel and a flax wheel stood ready to be used, and the large loom with its many wooden tools was in a corner. In another corner was the bucking tub

for washing. Buck was a word originating in the old country, meaning lye or suds for washing, but often referring to the clothes themselves. Chair forms (backless chairs), benches and stools made up the remaining equipment of a room that served the whole family the year through.

Here, too, was the bed in those first hard years. A very primitive one was fastened to the wall with heavy hinges, and was let down when used. This was called a let-down bed, a bed press, a jack-bed or a folding bed, and was the forerunner of the more elaborate beds which shut into the wall with folding doors, out of sight during the day. The name slaw-bank was another name used for the early beds, from the Dutch word, *sloap-banche,* meaning a sleeping bench. Children doubtless slept with parents, but later there appeared the trundle bed, or truckle bed, which had short legs and low posts and could be slid under the big bed. Another low-posted bed was the one used in the garret, which could stand under the eaves and was called the "hiredman's bed." No doubt it dates from a later time.

Mattresses of straw, oak leaves, beech-tree leaves, corn shucks or cattails were all that was afforded until feathers were possible, coming from wild geese and later from domestic geese

(*Left*) ATTRACTIVE CUPBOARD WITH DOME-SHAPED TOP, AND CURVED SHELVES MAKES A PLEASANT CORNER AT GREENWOOD PLACE.

THREE CUPBOARDS IN SLOPING WALL OF CHIMNEY FIT SNUGLY OVER THE FIREPLACE OF GREENWOOD PLACE. NOTE BAKE OVEN WITH IRON DOOR COVER AND ASH OVEN BELOW. *Paul W. Savage.*

AN OLD-TIME ROPE TIGHTENER USED IN STRINGING CORD BEDS. THE SLOTTED END TWISTED THE CORD WHILE THE PIN HELD IT TIGHT UNTIL END WAS SECURELY KNOTTED.

and chickens. The beds were corded with heavy rope, which was tightened with a forked implement of wood that took up the slack rope.

When more wealth and better living became the general thing, beds were made that harmonized with other fine furniture. There were fourposter beds and canopy beds of mahogany, first coming from across the water; later, beds of maple or pine or cherry were made by craftsmen in the new country. Elaborate carving and beautiful workmanship characterize these beds.

Bed clothing was handmade from the flax and wool grown and raised on the land, and block chintz and calico were made into quilts, comforters and counterpanes, while handmade netting covered the canopies and hung from the rails. The canopy overhead was called a tester. Bolsters and featherbeds were piled onto the rope beds to help keep the occupants warm; for the canopy bed, curtains were drawn to keep out the cold.

From the rafters of the old kitchen, or "hall," hung strings of dried apples and dried

PADDLE-SHAPED FEATHER BED SMOOTHER WAS USED TO SMOOTH A BED AFTER IT HAD BEEN TOSSED IN MAKING.

pumpkins, dried herbs and seed corn with the husks turned back and braided or "traced." The ears of corn were called "hands."

Such is the description of the old halls with their contents. Artists have portrayed those congested rooms, and perhaps no picture is more

ANOTHER VIEW OF THE ONONDAGA COUNTY CABIN SHOWING TURN-UP BED, CORNER CUPBOARD, HUTCH TABLE, AND DOZENS OF OTHER FURNISHINGS IN KEEPING WITH THE TIMES.

familiar than that by H. W. Pierce, painted in the nineteenth century and called "A New England Kitchen One Hundred Years Ago." Much history is gathered from the old prints that depict the life and homes of the early pioneers.

The room on the opposite side of the entry, known as the parlor, the "best room" or the company bedroom, contained a bed, tables, sea chests and chairs. The sea chests had come over with the owners and were used to hold the few pieces of wearing apparel and bedding; the chairs were described as "joyned," and doubtless were chairs with backs, seats and rungs instead of the backless forms, or stools. Here, too, was a desk, a warming pan of copper or brass, band boxes and other wooden receptacles. Some writers have said that the mistress slept in this parlor bedroom, but the small fireplace afforded little heat and in all probability the bed in the hall offered more comfort. One can easily see the need of the enclosed canopy bed in such a room as the company bedroom, with no comfort from the shallow fireplace.

It is sometimes stated that the early New

England families extended their houses laterally, but this is not strictly true, for some of the earliest New England homes, such as the Fairbanks house in Dedham, built in 1636, the Parson Capen house in Topsfield, built in 1683, both in Massachusetts, and the Jethro Coffin house in Nantucket, built in 1686, and many more, had a second floor.

The first addition to the two-room house with a loft or attic was a lean-to, a room built at the back of the house, with a fireplace opening into the main central chimney, thus making three openings in the one chimney. This fireplace was a large one, corresponding to the one in the kitchen. The lean-to was but one story, or occasionally two stories, the roof being a continuation of the main roof of the house. The addition appeared to lean against the main part of the house, which gave it the name of lean-to; the earlier name was "two-fall." The modern name, salt box, has been used for such a house with the addition, probably because the old salt boxes had a sloping cover and resembled a house with a sloping roof.

The lean-to, because of its large fireplace, was used as a work room to alleviate the hall of the many daily chores which fell to the lot of the women folk such as butter- and cheese-making, weaving, soap-making, candle-dipping, dyeing and washing. Sometimes part of the lean-to was partitioned off as a small bedroom, with no heat but that from the larger workroom. In New England this small room was sometimes used as a "borning room" or family sitting room.

Later the attic was finished off and used as

A second generation demanded a larger house and the structure was made into two rooms downstairs, with entry between, two finished bedrooms above and a lean-to, all of these using the central chimney, which was made larger to accommodate more rooms. One fireplace and its side bake oven served the grandparents, and another fireplace with its recessed back and an oven in the back part of the chimney served father, mother and children. Still another generation and another made changes with jogs,

TWO FIREPLACES IN THE SIMON WILLARD HOUSE, WHICH WAS BUILT IN 1659. HERE CAN BE SEEN TWO POSITIONS OF THE OVENS. (*Left*) OVEN IS IN THE REAR. (*Right*) BAKE OVEN IS AT THE SIDE.

two bedrooms, and this brought about the four-room house with an attic atop it all, but still having the one-story or two-story lean-to with a sloping part on the second floor used as an attic.

The Simon Willard house in Still River, once part of Lancaster, Massachusetts, is a unique example of how the houses underwent change. It was in 1659 that Simon Willard was assigned as commander-in-chief to a group in Lancaster to see that there was proper protection from the Indians. He and his family were given a house and many acres of land in a near-by section. The house had been built by a John Tinker, and had one room and a loft above. The fireplace measured ten feet wide. The loft was reached by a ladder, the top of which rested in a hole cut in the ceiling of the lower room; the opening can be seen today but is covered with floor boards.

wings and a second chimney in the rear addition, with a built-in set kettle in the cellar. It was then that the roof of the main part of the house was raised and the lean-to was taken away. But today, up in the attic, one can see the end beams that served for the slanting side of the lean-to, and there are hewn-out spaces in each old rafter of the new roof where the other lean-to beams had once been set into the timbers. The loft was thus changed into a large attic with two windows, one at either end.

More hands in the family made it possible to build larger homes or to change the attic into four finished rooms with a loft above. It is interesting to note shorter window frames in some of the early two-story houses, made to correspond to the lower ceiling of the second floor. Economy seemed to be considered before comfort for the family who must sleep in that upper

AN OLD ARISTOCRAT, THIS FINE HOME WAS BUILT WITH BRICK ENDS AND CLAPBOARDS FRONT AND REAR. NOTE SHEDS CONNECTING BARN TO HOUSE, AND THE FOUR CHIMNEYS. *Paul W. Savage.*

floor. But the low room was a heat-saving proposition, even though the small fireplaces in the upper chambers gave little heat. In later years, when cast iron appeared, registers were set into the floors and the heat rose from below, adding some scant comfort. Sometimes eavesdroppers upstairs listened to conversation carried on below. It is interesting to note here that the word eavesdropper originally meant to stand under the eaves to listen to what was being said inside the house.

Sheds, jogs and ells were added as the need arose, with extra space for windows to give light and air. The bedrooms on the second floor were named by their location over the lower rooms, such as hall chamber, meaning over the hall or kitchen, parlor chamber, ell chamber and shed chamber. The nursery rhyme says, "upstairs, downstairs, in my lady's chamber," and a lady's

chamber, as such, has always been in the Fairbanks house in Dedham.

Another step in building was to make a four-room house with chimneys at the two ends. This really was joining the one-room house with the wall chimney to a similar house, end to end, with an entry between and two rooms above, each with a fireplace on the outside wall. This was an extravagant way of building, for the chimney on the outside wall allowed for a fireplace only on one side of it. If a lean-to was added to such a house, a third chimney was built in that addition.

This brought about the brick-end houses, with clapboards front and back. When a chimney of brick was built at the side of the room, setting timbers and clapboards against the chimney called for skillful construction work. It was easier to continue the brickwork and make the entire wall of brick; and with bricks becoming more and more plentiful, the brick-end houses were not uncommon. Then the next natural step was to make all four sides of brick.

(*Above*) First part of the Wayside Inn to be built was a two room structure in 1702 later increased to four rooms in 1716.

(*Right*) Tavern section of Wayside Inn as remodled with additions in 1746. Situated in South Sudbury, Massachusetts.

As a family increased in size and the children married, more rooms were added to the old house and the several families lived under one roof. This saved the expense of building a new house, providing wood for more fireplaces and providing more food for families living separately. It also gave additional man power, which each household needed to carry on the daily living and for defense against the Indians. Some of the houses appear to be two or even three small houses with a common wall, each addition having its own chimney and fireplace. The Fairbanks house in Dedham (page 29) shows this type of house, each generation having put on an addition and made a few changes.

The former Wayside Inn at South Sudbury, Mass., is an example of how rooms were added on to the original structure. The first part was a two-room structure, one room on the first floor and a room above, built by Samuel How (with no E) sometime between 1700 and 1702. The chimney was at the West end of the house, against which lay a narrow, winding staircase to the second floor. A few years later, a son David How built two more rooms at the other side of the chimney, enlarging the entry and adding to the chimney to provide fireplaces in those two additional rooms.

Again an addition was made by building four rooms at the back, upstairs and downstairs, making an eight-room house. This was done by Ezekial Howe, a grandson. The central chimney gave way to two chimneys, between the rooms either side of the hallway which ran from front to back.

From the study of old records during the restoration in 1955, it was found that when the structure had four rooms, two downstairs and two upstairs, one of the front rooms was used as a bar room for stage-coach travellers. It was then that the sign HOW TAVERN was hung. About 1746, with the additional rooms and the change in chimney structure, the sign then displayed a bright red horse that read THE RED HORSE TAVERN. A ball room, all-important

in taverns and Inns, is supposed to have been in one of the upper rooms in the back part. When Longfellow visited the Tavern and when his famous TALES were published (1863), the name became THE WAYSIDE INN.

With the adding of the back four rooms, a new roof was built, a gambrel roof, rising above and in place of the old sloping roof. In rebuilding the Inn after the devastating fire in 1955, the framework of the sloping roof of the first two and second two rooms was built within the gambrel roof, to show the structure of that first house.

The illustration on page 53 of the fireplace in the Wayside Inn is not in the original eight-room structure. From pictures that were found among the old records, it was shown that a barn

Sturdy rafters of the Greenwood Place are held together by eight-inch wooden pegs driven in with a heavy mallet. *Paul W. Savage.*

stood closely adjoining the house. In later years it was moved and placed as part of the eight-room structure. In that, a large kitchen was built with a fireplace and a bedroom above, reached by narrow stairs with high risers. This addition leads from a smaller kitchen with fireplace that was in the eight-room structure of Ezekial Howe, behind the bar room.

A ballroom was a necessary room in all taverns, for balls were frequently given for guests and visitors of high rank. The arched ceiling appears to have been the proper way of constructing the room, for this allowed heat to rotate and thus make the room warmer. Around the walls were boxed-in seats where the wraps were kept.

A fiddler's seat is occasionally seen — a round, raised extension, with a rail; here the fiddler stood as he called the dances. Window leaves or shutters were at the windows, to help further in keeping the room warm. Early ballrooms had tin sconces for candles on the side walls, or hanging in chandeliers or candle-beams from the ceiling.

In those days houses and barns were "raised," a term not generally understood today, though "raisings" have been carried on in some country districts in the last generation. In erecting a house, the first step was to build the central chimney of field stones or granite boulders if

they were readily available. If they were not at hand, then bricks were used, which were brought from a kiln that was usually located nearby. The entire chimney, complete with fireplaces and ovens, was carefully planned and was built from the ground up with detailed exactitude.

A framework for the house was then put together on the ground, of planed oak logs which were named according to the position they were to take in the structure. The sills lay on the ground (previous to cellars), and also on the ground were laid the posts for the four corners of the house and doorway, with transverse beams running across. These beams were called "summers," from the word sumpter, which means something that carries weight, and these "summers" carried the weight of the second floor. Girts and girders ran from the three or more summers, and rafters were slanted for the attic and lean-to, meeting the ridge pole at the top.

With the help of the entire community, and with ropes and pulleys, one side after another of the new house or barn was lifted into an upright position. Then, the four sides set into place, the rafters for the roof were put on and the ridge pole laid. The entire structure was put together with large hand-hewn pegs, driven in with a heavy mallet called a beetle.

Community spirit ran high at a house-raising, and after the ridge pole had been crowned with much rum, a feast followed for the entire group. There was never any hesitation about the community joining in to help in these undertakings.

Shelters were erected for the first animals that arrived, and when hay and grain were cut and ready to store, barns were added to the ever-increasing number of buildings. In New England the barns were built at right angles to the house, to which they were joined by sheds, and this made a sheltered yard. The barn could be reached without going out-of-doors in inclement weather.

In Pennsylvania and New York state, barns were very large, showing that farming was of vast importance. In Pennsylvania, a threshing floor was not an uncommon thing. It was made with small spaces between the floor boards through which the grain dropped as it was beaten from the stalks. The South, with its many outbuildings, had barns which were built to protect livestock and grains against heat rather than snow. All barns had a large open space in the middle for unloading hay and for threshing grain on the floor.

A MALLET, ALSO CALLED A BEETLE, HAD MANY USES AROUND THE COLONIAL HOUSE. THIS ONE WAS MADE OF ASH OR MAPLE BURL.

ADDITIONS WERE INVARIABLY BUILT ON TO THE EARLY AMERICAN HOUSE. (*Below*) SHEDS CONNECTING HOUSE WITH BARN. (*Below, right*) HIPPED-ROOF HOUSE AND SHEDS ARE JOINED TOGETHER WITH A JOG.

Live stock was brought to the new country about 1630. In the spring of the year it was pastured on the common, the small tract of land set apart in each town to which the live stock could be driven to graze. The common is dealt with more fully in Chapter Five.

In the course of time the women of the family had a hand in planning the house, and the congestion of the kitchen was relieved. Then came the pantry, milk room and buttery. It would be hard to tell the exact period of their appearance, but one may be sure that the pantry was added first. The word pantry comes from the French word *pain,* meaning bread. The pantry was a small room leading out of the kitchen, sometimes with a window; it had shelves, cupboards and a sink of wood or soapstone.

A well was usually located in the yard not far from the house. The old well with its well-sweep is still a picturesque adjunct of houses built in the seventeenth and eighteenth centuries. The bucket was hoisted on a heavy rope by means of the sweep, a long pole balanced on a fulcrum. The sweep was made of white birch, stripped of its bark, and would last about seventeen years. If the bark had been left on, the sweep would have lasted about one year. Mechanical devices with wheel and cranks came when iron products appeared. The bucket was strong and durable, of heavy oak staves and iron bands — one poet put such a bucket into song. There were buckets with trap doors set in with leather hinges.

In the Simon Willard house, a well eighteen feet deep was in the dooryard, and when a later generation added a wing to the four-room house, to be used as a kitchen, the addition lay directly over the well. A windlass for the bucket was built in the loft of this wing and still stands intact. It has a wheel five feet in diameter, made of two rims of wood and two sets of spokes put together with blocks that form a groove to hold the well cord. The axle is sturdy, ten inches in diameter and five feet long, and at the end is a heavy cylindrical block to balance the wheel. The rope attached to the bucket came through a hole in the floor of the kitchen and up through

AN OLD WELL SWEEP RAISES THE BUCKET SEVENTEEN FEET FROM THE BOTTOM OF THIS BOXED-IN WELL.

a hole in the ceiling to the windlass. The windlass took the weight of the bucket, which could be hoisted with little effort. Today, the well is covered, the holes are boarded over and the windlass stands in silent inactivity.

Remains of wooden pipes and troughs and pipes made of soapstone show that water also was brought into the houses to a pump. Some kitchen sinks received water from a near-by stream, which was piped into the house, and it was a never-ending supply. Such a stream still feeds the sink of an old house not far from Greenfield, Massachusetts, its force never having been broken even in dry seasons, throughout five generations.

In the pantry there was a mixed array of utensils. A few came from across the water, and these were of pewter, iron, brass and wood; but when wood was right at hand and so abundant, utensils and implements of this material were

soon fashioned with a jackknife, and often according to the suggestions of the women folk. Wooden utensils were easily replaced when worn, and new demands brought new tools from season to season.

Boxes, both round and oval, for spices, meals, herbs, sugar and "sody" (soda); buckets for milk and water and the "sugaring-off" season; mortars and pestles to crush the various commodities as they came to the house in coarse form, brought by whaling vessels; rolling pins and cooky rollers and the pie crimper for the many cookies and pies that took long hours to make — all these tools were in the pantry. The word cooky comes from the Dutch word *koekje,* which is the diminutive form of *koek,* meaning cake; and also from the French word *coket.*

Chopping bowls and the chopping knife, fashioned by hand from a piece of wood and a scrap of steel, were always busy. The most beautiful bowls are those made from the burl on a tree. This is a wart that grows on many trees, a mild tumor, and because normal growth has been checked the grain of the wood is broken. The shape of the burl suggested a bowl, first to the Indians and then to the white man. Maple and ash burls were used, for they are tough— others are punky and porous. Many utensils beside the bowls were made from the burl, such as mortars, butter workers, salts, scoops, dippers and urns.

Brooms were made from a birch sapling, as the Indians did. They were splintered and tied and used for many purposes. The long one saw service at the hearth and on floors; those

measuring about two feet were used to scrub the kettles and pots and to brush out the bake oven after a fire had been made to heat the oven; and last but not least, there was the tiny splintered broom for beating eggs of wild turkeys or of domestic hens and geese. This broom, called a whisk, measured not more than five inches. Still another beater, and one a bit more sanitary, was the small birch twig, slashed at the lower end. Because of the slashes, it acted as a sort of beater when the twig was twirled between the hands in whisking eggs or whipping cream.

A MAPLE BURL WITH THE BARK PEELED OFF. TO MAKE A BOWL, THE BURL WAS DILIGENTLY BURNED AND CARVED UNTIL PROPER SHAPE WAS ACHIEVED.

(*Above*) WOODEN BUTTER BOXES WERE MADE WITH STAVES AND HOOP-LOCKED LAPS TO ALLOW FOR BOXES' EXPANSION WITH MOIST BUTTER. (*Right*) THESE HANDMADE MEAL BOXES WERE FASTENED TOGETHER WITH HANDWROUGHT NAILS AND WOODEN PEGS.

The utensils for the table for mealtime were also of wood. Plates of wood were called trenchers, from the old French word meaning to cut or carve. For a trencher was originally a board or plate on which the food was carved. They were both round and square in shape. Custom required two people to eat from the same plate. Indentations for salt and condiments in each corner characterized the trenchers that came from the old country, which were square in shape, while the new trenchers of the pioneers were round and made on the lathe. Another custom was to turn the plate over and eat the dessert on the under side, so that the two sides were spoken of as the "dinner side" and the "pie side." Some plates from England had inscriptions and verses around the edge, especially those that were round.

Pitchers were called noggins. They were passed from mouth to mouth, the common drink being cider. The word noggin dates back to Old English, and means a block of wood, from which the noggin was shaped on the lathe and by hand. Eating bowls for stews and porridges and the large family salt bowl completed the array of eating utensils that stood on the plank table of oak, resting on trestles.

The wood used in making these various kitchen utensils and receptacles was pine, birch, maple (both bird's-eye and curly), ash, hickory, beech, chestnut, woods from various fruit trees and the heavy lignum vitae brought to the new country on whaling vessels, which went out with masts, bricks, salt and other goods, and brought back many things that did not exist in a country that had been wilderness not long before. To provide much of this kitchen ware, there were coopers and dish turners with shops in the ell of a house or out in the yard. Each season saw the cooper traveling from village to village, mending and repairing wooden ware such as buckets, tubs, churns and tankards. Peddlers carried wooden ware in their packs.

The second important addition to the house was the milk room, where the butter and cheese were made — butter during the winter months and cheese in the summertime. The utensils for making those two important foods were large and bulky and took up much space — butter churns, butter trays of wood and pottery, cheese presses, drainers, racks and boxes, as well as tools for working butter and making cheese. A cheese closet hung on the wall, a set of shelves with a frame door covered with cheesecloth. This thin gauze had no special name until it was used on cheese closets, when it came to be called cheesecloth.

Cheese presses were of varied sorts, from those that pressed out one cheese to those that had pulleys and weights and held three cheeses. Some presses were built into the room, fastened to the floor. When the equipment for making cheese and butter was taken away from the kitchen and put in a milk room or a cheese room, it gave more space for the daily kitchen work.

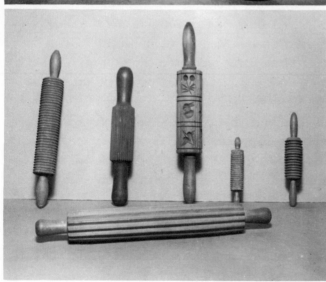

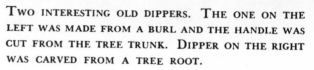
(*From top to bottom*) TWO LARGE BOWLS MADE
FROM BURLS. THE ONE ON THE LEFT WAS USED TO
HOLD GREASE, HENCE ITS DARK COLOR. THE OTHER
BOWL WAS MADE BY AN INDIAN IN 1803 AND WAS
USED IN SERVING FOOD. BELOW APPEAR VARIOUS
WOODEN UTENSILS EACH OF WHICH HAD AN IMPOR-
TANT PLACE IN THE EARLY AMERICAN HOUSEHOLD:
SPOON HOLDER OF MAPLE WOOD, NOGGIN, AND SMALL
SUGAR BOWL; LARGE TRENCHER OVER 200 YEARS OLD,
A PLATE, AND EATING BOWLS; AND SIX COOKY ROLLERS
SHOWING DESIGNS IMPRESSED ON THE DOUGH.

The third room was perhaps not needed
by every housewife, but if it was possible, the
buttery was added to relieve the congestion of
the pantry. The word buttery is of Old French
origin, and meant a place for keeping bottles
or casks. The buttery of the early settlers (colloquially pronounced buttry) held more than
casks, for in it was the overflow of the pantry.
There was the barrel of maple-sugar cakes, the
keg of vinegar, the barrels of meal and of soft
soap, the dye tub, the washtubs and the implements for washing, such as the dolly, which was
a scrubbing stick and pounder, the washboards
and a smoothing stick for pressing. Here, too,
were the bowls of all descriptions, the sap buckets and tubs, the keg for rum and water to take
to the fields when working, the powdering tub
for salting down meats, the candle-dipping
equipment — a motley array it was that found
its way into the buttery.

Before these various rooms were added,
there seems to have been one small storeroom or
closet, called a larder, equipped with shelves,
racks and hooks. It was away from the heat of
the big fireplace, and therefore a cold room.
In this, food was stored before it was cooked, or
heated for eating — such food as meat, fish,
game, pies, apple butter, and bean porridge.
Sometimes the larder had a window for light
and air. (See Chapter Five.)

As to the house structure, when it changed
in size, the style of the roof changed also. There
was an old law which placed a tax on the second
story, so to avoid this the roof was made a gambrel roof, with two slopes to each side of the

(*Left*) Gambrel-roofed original house and ell were built in 1694. (*Center*) Larger addition, known as The Manse, was erected in 1768. This house is located in Old Deerfield, Massachusetts. (*Right*) Another fine gambrel-roofed dwelling in Old Deerfield.

roof, one of which might be longer than the other, or both of equal length. This, a style of roof-building in Holland, allowed more space under the eaves. Two windows, one at either end of the attic, gave light, and because of them, there could be two rooms, with a partition between them. Thus the upper floor, considered as an attic, served somewhat the purpose of a second story.

The overhang of the roof of the early houses is very noticeable. This was copied, like many other styles, from houses across the water, and the reasons for it are varied. Some historians say that the overhang protected those walking on the streets from rain; others that it protected the walls of the house, which were not so solidly built then — often clapboards and shingles did not lap sufficiently to give complete protection from the elements. Still another theory is that they were built this way so that peek holes in the under part of the overhang could allow the family to watch from the attic, whither they had fled from the Indians. All these are likely reasons; and overhangs continued to be popular for many years. They were sometimes built only on the front, sometimes on the front and two sides, or on all four sides. Ornamental drops were often hung from the corners.

In spite of the tax on the second story, houses were built with a second story by the middle of the seventeenth century. This gave eight rooms and an attic, the chimney in the center allowing for six fireplaces, three on a floor. Those on the second floor were small in size, being for heating only. But they actually gave little heat — Benjamin Franklin stated that five-sixths of the heat went up the chimney, and this fact led him to invent stoves with pipes fitting into the chimney hole. Then began another era in the homes.

A still further change in the style of roofs came in the hip roof. This has four equal slopes on the four sides of the house, with a flat roof on top. If the house is not square, but rectangular in shape, the four slopes come to a ridge, the opposite sides being alike.

The flat roof brought about the fenced-in space on top of the house, which was known as the captain's walk or the widow's walk. It was especially popular in seaport towns, where a view of the ocean was afforded and the families could watch for the incoming ships.

To extend the number of sleeping rooms, windows were thrown out in the gambrel roof. These were called dormer windows because of their use in the sleeping rooms, the French word *dormir* meaning to sleep. They were put in the lower part of the roof, near the floor, and only at the front of the house. The two end windows remained the same. Gable windows were also added, being much more pretentious in structure, allowing more space than merely that of a window.

The hip roof went through the same transformation as the gambrel roof, with dormer windows added. But in this case, windows were added on all four sides, since there were four rooms partitioned off. No other windows except these dormer windows were in the attic of the houses with hip roofs.

Another type of roof which became popular was the gable roof. It was this type of roof that brought about the House of the Seven Gables in Salem, Massachusetts. This style, too, was copied from the old houses across the water. A gable was built on the side of the house, beginning at the eaves and going up to the ridge of the roof, corresponding in lines with the end of the old sloping roof. In this gable a window was built. The structure was more difficult to build and the style was not generally used, nor did it remain popular long.

While the houses were changing and the roofs were correspondingly different, the chimneys, too, underwent changes. The first two-room house had one chimney in the center, the same chimney serving the lean-to when that was added. Or there were two chimneys, one in each of the two rooms, built into the outside wall. This, as has been mentioned, brought about the brick ends to the houses, the front and back of the house being shingled or covered with clapboards. Sometimes the chimney was built partly inside and partly outside the wall. This arrangement gave only one opening to the chimney, one on each floor.

A more practical way of placing two chimneys was to build them between the front and back room, either side of the entry. This gave a fireplace for each of the four rooms, the two front rooms being the best rooms, and the back rooms being used for bedroom and kitchen, the kitchen having a large fireplace and oven. The four upper chambers each had a fireplace. This arrangement of the two chimneys allowed more space for the entry in the middle of the house, and then it was called a hallway and often ran the entire length of the house. This type of house had been in general use in the South at all times, but in the North the cold seasons did not invite large hallways.

Still another arrangement was to add a third chimney at the back of the house, for the kitchen. With this, the two end fireplaces continued to be built into the outside walls, serving the two front rooms, while the third fireplace was for the two rooms at the back, with an opening in each room.

A fourth chimney came as the next step, one being in the outside wall of each of the four rooms. This necessitated a fifth chimney for the kitchen if it was in a wing, and this chimney, having two openings, was also used as an extra workroom at the back.

Such houses, with four or five chimneys, were built in prosperous times, when more rooms were needed for entertaining and for guests. While building chimneys was a difficult task that took much material, it would seem as if a prevailing style was considered ahead of the hard labor of building. One chimney of a home in Salem, built in the late eighteenth century, is said to have contained 25,000 bricks, which were counted as the chimney was being torn down.

In the South, the kitchen was not always in the main part of the house, but out in the slaves' quarters, not too far from the house. This gave the slaves a type of house such as was built in

(*Below*) THIS GEORGIAN HOUSE BUILT BY CAPTAIN WILLIAM NICKELS IN WISCASSET, MAINE, IS A NEW ENGLAND CLASSIC. (*Right*) THE WENTWORTH-GARDNER HOUSE, BUILT IN 1760, IS A PORTSMOUTH, NEW HAMPSHIRE, LANDMARK. *Clayton Jenks.*

THE FAMOUS OLD HOUSE OF SEVEN GABLES IN
SALEM, MASSACHUSETTS, WAS THE SETTING FOR
HAWTHORNE'S IMMORTAL STORY OF THE SAME
NAME. *Maynard Workshop.*

New England in the earliest days, having a central chimney with rooms around it. Often the kitchen was built as a separate building connected with the main house by a passageway. Slaves were the common thing in the South, and hard labor was never done by either the menfolks or the womenfolks, the gentlemen or the ladies. With an outside kitchen, all food had to be carried some distance to the dining room, and the question might arise about the food being "piping hot." (The author has a large coffin-shaped tray, with its original design in gold and color, which carried food from the kitchen in the slave quarters to the house, in a Connecticut seaport town.)

The entrance to the early houses was without any protection and the door sill rested on the ground, with a huge flat stone for a doorstep. The first addition to the front door was in the nature of a stoop, a small covered platform with a bench at each side of the door. The Dutch, who called it "stoep," brought this to the new country from their homeland. Lattice-work or blinds were put behind the seats for protection.

Our word "piazza" comes from the Italian word meaning a square or a market place. This was adopted by America, and any open addition to the house, whether at front, side or back, became a piazza. The English brought the word "veranda" from India, and it originally meant an outdoor sitting room. "Porch" is another commonly used word in America, coming from the Latin *porticus* and the French *porche*.

The convenience of the piazza, veranda or porch was realized, and by the eighteenth century every home, whether of simple design or of elaborate plan, had an outdoor addition. The pillared house of the Georgian period had an upper piazza, often with an iron railing, and in many cases the addition was not for use but for ornamentation. The homely use of the piazza, however, became very important, and the piazza was not only a gathering place for the family and friends and a storing place for odds and ends, but even a place for the clothesline and the weekly washing.

As the population increased, and more and more men were sent for from across the water, to help build houses, the styles displayed greater wealth. By the beginning of the eighteenth century, wealth lay in the seacoast towns, where shipping was the main occupation. Building ships and operating merchant vessels that sailed the high seas brought much money, even though the business entailed many losses, fluctuating as it did from season to season. Another occupation which afforded wealth was that of the salt industry. The new country was rich in salt mines, and from these as well as from the ocean, salt was obtained and sold both at home and abroad.

Another side of this period from the beginning through the middle of the eighteenth century was the breaking away from the control of England, living more independently and no longer acknowledging that England was lord. This gave more freedom in ways of living and in manners, in spite of the fact that strict laws continued to be enforced in the various communities in the new settlements.

Building material varied. The Dutch often made each side of the house from different materials — stones, brick, stucco, clapboards, shingles and even stucco put over rubble, which was nothing but broken stones and glass. In New England wood was used almost entirely, with an occasional house of brick, field stone or flat stone. Brick was used in Pennsylvania, Delaware, Maryland and Virginia, in spite of the fact that there was plenty of timber. The bricks in the South were made from clay and from adobe, material at hand. The combination of wooden houses with brick-ends came to be popular, and all-stone houses as well as all-brick houses are fairly common in every section.

The styles of architecture continued to be taken from the old country, and this period of wealth produced a house of the Georgian type, a name given to a style of architecture during the time of four King Georges of England, 1714-1830. These houses were very fine and unusually striking; elaborateness characterized them all. Roofs and chimneys mattered not — everything tended toward decoration, inside and out. Colonnaded porticoes, with beautiful doorways, having narrow windows above and at the sides, and graced with a brass knocker; windows with ornamental lintels above; cornices and pillars, quoined corners and an elaborate captain's walk or a fenced-in roof — all of these added to the effect. Stone steps led to the piazza, and wrought-iron railings by the steps and in an upper balcony appeared as other items of beauty. Spacious grounds were marked out and fenced with either wooden pickets or iron rails, and flower gardens became more pretentious.

THIS POST-COLONIAL HOUSE SHOWS AN ELABORATE BUT NOT UNPLEASING USE OF PIAZZAS AND IRON RAILINGS, A RARE SIGHT IN NEW ENGLAND.

Within the house, the same lavishness was evident; there was wainscotting and paneling in the hallways, stairways with mahogany baluster and fluted spindles, carved newell posts, a window seat on the upper landing. The rooms were paneled, or finished with elaborate wainscotting, and heavy paneled doors had hand-wrought hardware, sometimes of brass; windows had deep sills and wooden shutters or window leaves; fireplaces were finished with colored tiles sent from across the water, and there were elaborate accessories on the hearth. Wallpapers were of rich designs, and hand-blocked. All of these things characterized the homes of wealth in the last part of the eighteenth century.

At this period fine furniture filled the rooms — Chippendale, Sheraton and Hepplewhite — and the glass and china were of the finest, much of it brought from foreign lands.

There was luxurious living and lavish entertainment and hospitality, offered by hosts and hostesses in fine silks, velvets, brocades and jewelry. This period was the peak of fine living and culture, and a far cry from life in the one-room house of the early settlers, carried on under hardships and struggles, not only with Nature but with the ever-dreaded Indians.

Each generation comes into changed environments and adapts its living to the problems which it has to face. Each century sees new developments and new ways of living, but ever in the background is the inheritance handed on by the hardy group of pioneers who landed on these shores, made their homes and lived their lives, explored and expanded into new territory, always the same courageous people who left the shores of the old country to venture into the unknown.

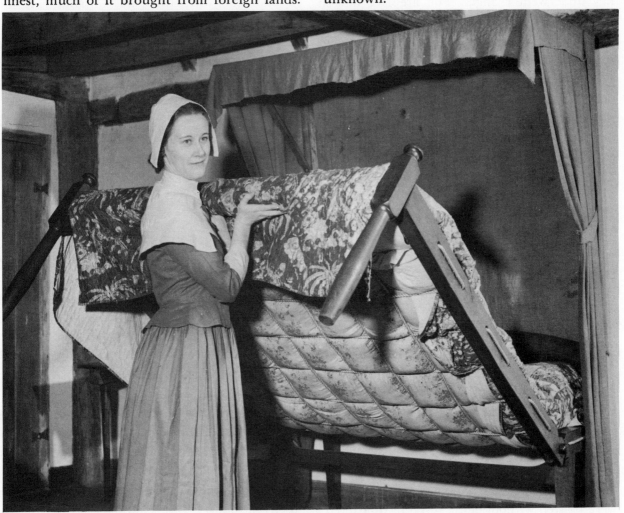

EARLY RARE TURN-UP BED IN THE OLD IRON WORKS HOUSE IN SAUGUS, MASSACHUSETTS. THIS HAS A NARROW CANOPY OVERHEAD.

II

Chimneys and Fireplaces--Heart of the Home

As the homes of the colonies changed from those of one room to the pretentious ones of the eighteenth century, so the structure of the chimney underwent changes. The fireplace offered both heat for comfort and heat for cooking, and with that in mind the early settlers planned in the building of them.

The word chimney originally meant the fireplace, and poets write of the "chimney corner" where sat both young and old, within the fireplace on the hearth. The word finally came to mean the entire structure from the base to the outside projection above the roof. Later, the term chimney shaft was used for the projection above the roof.

The chimney of the wigwams and the first one-room house was built of field stones and thin slabs of stone taken from the surrounding land, and set with clay mixed with sand and grasses. The stones were laid in a shallow trench in the ground as a foundation for the chimney. The opening of the fireplace varied in width from six to eight feet, and an occasional one was ten feet wide. The depth was five or six feet, and it was as high as it was deep. Above the fireplace, the chimney tapered, leaving sufficient room for the flue, until it was the size of the outside shaft.

In fireplaces of such size, logs six or eight feet long could be burned, and whole animals were roasted without being sliced or quartered. Wood was abundant — in fact, abundant to excess — and fireplaces were the only means of heat, so the large fireplace, accommodating the massive logs, was a necessity, besides allowing for cooking and roasting in great quantities. At a later time, when wood was not abundant, the size of the fireplaces became much smaller.

The part of the chimney above the roof was first made of wood, as related in the previous chapter, but only for a short time. Sticks, laid two by two, were daubed with clay inside and out. As the clay dried and crumbled the wood was exposed to the heat of the fire, so that after many houses were burned down, the law prohibiting the use of wood in building chimneys was passed.

Nature provided material for bricks in the clay found in the soil by the shores of the ocean and in the beds of rivers. This was mixed with sand and water· and baked in kilns, making. bricks. In New Jersey, adobe was sometime a substitute for brick. This was made from sun-baked blocks of marl, which was another type of soil made up of lime, clay and sand, and had been used by Indians and other races in the Southwest, where such soil was found extensively. No exact date can be given when bricks were first used in building chimneys, but it was approximately at the end of the seventeenth century.

Field stone and flat stones continued to be used in houses and chimneys, even though bricks could be transported long distances. In clearing the land for building, great quantities

PLAN OF CHIMNEY STRUCTURE. NOTE BAKE OVEN AND ASH OVEN AT LEFT OF MAIN FIREPLACE, AND SMALL FIREPLACES IN SIDE ROOM AND ON SECOND FLOOR. SUCH A CHIMNEY WAS BUILT OF BRICK OR FIELD STONES.

45

of stones and rocks were dug up, and ridding the land of them was vital. Cellar foundation walls were built of huge boulders or stone slabs, so heavy and massive that it took the strength of men and oxen to haul them and set them into place. Each section of the country offered slight variation of material for foundations. Stone walls began to be laid for boundary lines and provided another means of using the great amount of stones and shale.

The ruins of an old chimney show how carefully the structure was planned and built, from the foundation to the top. A few such

ALL THAT REMAINS OF AN OLD HOUSE AFTER A FIRE ARE THE RUINS OF A FINE CHIMNEY. (*Above*). THE DOOR TO THE SMOKE ROOM WAS APPARENTLY LOCATED UNDER A STAIRWAY.

(*Right*) AN INDICATION OF THE SIZE OF THE DWELLING CAN BE GAINED FROM THE NUMBER OF FIREPLACES IN THE CHIMNEY.

(*Below*) NOTICE WOODEN LINTEL SET INTO BRICKS OVER EACH FIREPLACE.

ruins are left today, but the houses and their chimneys are fast disappearing.

Briefly, the chimney structure, from base to top of shaft, was as follows: first, the base of varying types, with indentations for wine or preserves; supports at ceiling of cellar for hearthstone above; then fireplaces and bake oven; slope called the shoulder, a place for cupboards; smoke ovens or ham rooms in chimney in any convenient location (from cellar to attic);

46

UNSHEATHED BRICK CHIMNEY RISES INSIDE HOUSE TO THE ROOF. SQUARE PROJECTIONS AT SIDE OF CHIMNEY ARE FOR FIREPLACES FACING INTO ROOMS ON THE SECOND FLOOR.

second floor, shallow fireplaces; above ridgepole a ledge in the chimney called a dripstone, preventing water from seeping into the attic (forerunner of modern flashing) ; sloping chimney to outside chimney shaft.

It is rare to find a chimney now with no sheathing around it in the entry, but such is the case in the William Hartwell house, in Lincoln, Massachusetts, once a part of Concord. Built between 1635 and 1639, the chimney is massive, with large fireplaces. In the entry, with no sheathing or wall protection, the chimney rises at the side of the staircase. The lower part is the width of the entry, then it tapers to the second floor, where the fireplaces are shallow. It continues to taper up to the shaft, but even there it is of no small size. The bricks form steps as they rise one layer upon another, and after three centuries of use the chimney still stands, a mute testimony of the hand work of our ancestors.

Perhaps the most varied part of the chimney structure was the base, built in the cellar, when excavations began to be made beneath the houses. Apparently the easiest one to make was that of field stones set or "puddled" in clay. This puddle, a mixture of clay and sand, was

SUPPORTING ARCH IN THE BASEMENT FOR ONE OF THE HUGE CHIMNEYS IN THE RUFUS PUTNAM HOUSE IN RUTLAND, MASSACHUSETTS. THE LARGEST STONES AVAILABLE WERE USED IN BUILDING THIS ARCH.

stones was set with puddle, it was held in place while drying with supports of wood. The last opening was filled with the shaped stone called the key, one such key in a two-hundred-year-old house being a slab of wood, instead of a stone, and running the entire fifteen-foot length of the archway.

Some archways in the chimney base were very shallow, while others were as high as seven or eight feet. In the Rufus Putnam house in Rutland, Massachusetts, at the base of two huge chimneys there are two arches fully seven feet high, built of stone. They stand as a wonderful example of work lasting these two centuries. The number of stones and the days of labor are left to the imagination.

In the same cellar in Rutland, an unusual item is the stairway to the first floor above. On a pair of stayers, two parallel sloping beams, rest beams that were either split or sawed on their diagonal, making a step ten inches wide and four feet long. It is a pleasant sensation to tread the old oak logs, for there is a spring in the wood that stones or bricks cannot give. Some of the cellars built in the eighteenth century were very deep, and that made a long flight of stairs leading to the floor above. In the early days, steps of stone sometimes led through the foundation from outdoors, and this was often the only means of reaching the cellar.

The Wayside Inn in South Sudbury, built in 1700, and the Fairbanks homestead in Dedham, built in 1636, have foundations of solid rock. Both the Wayside Inn and the Fairbanks house have one central chimney in the main part, to which additions have been made by following generations. The tavern of the Wayside Inn, built in 1716, has two chimneys, making three in all; while in the Fairbanks house there are two chimneys as it stands today.

In the John Stebbins house in Old Deerfield, built in 1772, there are two chimneys of field stone, with bases of different structure. In one there is a huge fireplace with a brick oven, and in the other a preserve closet. The cellar is eight feet six inches high. Heavy work, such as soap-making and wool-dyeing, was carried on in

used instead of the present-day mortar. At intervals of two or three feet, slabs of rock or thick oaken planks were set in to strengthen the structure, holding the weight of the stones or bricks evenly and preventing any settling. Some of the bases are as much as fifteen feet square.

The base of the chimney was often made as an arch, perhaps with the idea of saving stones but more likely to give a firmer support to the massive structure. The science of the arch is that each stone or brick supports the others when placed in the direction of the radii of the curve, the pressure of the whole being supported by the diagonal position of the bricks. Today, a framework is made, and the stones or bricks laid onto that; but in the old days, as each row of

shop, used by the village baker when he baked for many families, and it was here that the weekly pots of beans were brought and called for, with brown bread added.

The chimney in a house on the outskirts of Worcester, Massachusetts, with a brick base has a combination use. Half of it is a narrow preserve closet and the other half a smoke oven. The closet is lined on three sides with shelves, which extend to the ceiling. The oven or smoke room on the opposite side has a long, narrow door, set in two feet from the floor. Anyone smoking meat stepped into the opening, which was something a bit difficult to do. Six pairs of

THIS CHIMNEY BASE IN THE CELLAR OF AN OLD HOUSE CONTAINS A SMOKE OVEN WITH A WOODEN DOOR. (*Right*) VIEW OF OPPOSITE SIDE OF CHIMNEY BASE SHOWS DOOR TO PRESERVE CLOSET.

FLOORS OF EARLY HOUSES WERE OFTEN SUPPORTED BY BEAMS PLACED AROUND TOP OF CHIMNEY BASE. EXTRA HEAVY BEAMS SUPPORTED HEARTHSTONE.

the extra fireplace, as well as roasting whole animals, thus taking much confusion away from the main kitchen upstairs. The preserve closet is the size of a small room, three sides having rows of shelves and the fourth side taken up with the wide door which swings on hand-wrought iron hinges, with a heavy oaken lintel above. It is in this house that the attic, the length of the house and a story and a half high, was the meeting place for the women of the village who gathered to spin and weave and make garments.

Wright's Tavern in Concord, Massachusetts, built in 1747, has a huge foundation, with a fireplace and brick oven in the base of the chimney. Here in the cellar was the village bake

hooks, facing each other, were set into the ceiling, which is fully six feet from the floor; the hooks are eight inches long. On these, six hams could be smoked at one time. Or a whole hog could be hung in the smoke room on a pair of hooks. It might be thought that the occasional smoking of meat in this section would affect the temperature of the preserve closet on the other side of the brick wall; but since the heat for smoking was never intense, it is possible that the preserves were not affected.

The old Simon Willard house in Harvard, Massachusetts, went through its first change by having the chimney of the first one-room house made larger to serve a four-room house. The base of the chimney, eleven and a half feet square, is made of field stones, and in it is a preserve closet. But in the course of time, the chimney has been taken over for heating apparatus.

Many chimney bases of brick have an archway with stone slabs on the floor, and the archway space was used as a closet for storing. Usually one can see where a door once swung, the holes for hinges and latches still visible. Indentations in the sides of the foundations were used as shelves for bottles of wines. Wine was in general use, much of it imported until vineyards were planted by the colonists. And there was always plenty of barley and hops to be turned into brewed drinks. John Quincy Adams records in his dairy in the first part of the nineteenth century that he had a very elaborate meal at four o'clock in the afternoon, and he winds up by saying, "I drank Madeira at a great rate and found no inconvenience from it."

As bricks became more available for building, brickmakers were sent for, coming from England along with carpenters and other workmen who could help in building better homes. By the end of the seventeenth century or the beginning of the eighteenth, New Jersey and colonies farther south had acquired wealth through trading by ships, and it was at this period that brick-making was a thriving industry, the bricks sent to Bermuda in exchange for limestone to be used in mortar.

There were two kinds of brick, which, depending on their size and shape, were called Dutch and English. The bricks were made by descendants of Dutch and English settlers, and were patterned on the bricks made across the water. Some bricks were 4 by 8¼ inches, and 2⅝ inches thick; while others were 4 by 8 inches, and 2½ inches thick, the thinner ones being Dutch. All the bricks were roughly molded; some were underburned, others extremely hard-burned; and they were of many shades of color, making for more ornamentation when used.

Brickwork in time became more common in the Middle States and in the South, for those sections had less field stones with which to build. Another fact to consider is that some of the groups from European countries clung to the customs of the old countries in their building, while others broke away from the old and accepted the new conditions and improved upon them as the years went along. It took courageous and independent-minded people to break away from the strong inherited characteristics of their forebears.

As extra support for the weight of the kitchen fireplace and ovens, huge slabs of stone or squared logs were set in at the top of the base, just below the floor of the room above. These supports extended two or more feet on all four sides of the structure, making a platform to ease the strain of the floor timbers, which held the hearthstone.

The chimney tapered above the cellar foundation to the size of the fireplace on the first floor. The wood used in the great fireplace has been picturesquely described as "sweet-scented hickory, snapping chestnut, odiferous oak and reeking, fizzling ash." To lay a fire required much skill. "First a back log fifteen inches to twenty-four inches by five feet, imbedded in the ashes; then a top log; then a fore log; then a middle stick and then a heap of kindlings reaching from the bowels down to the bottom. A-top of all was a pyramid of smaller fragments artfully adjusted with spaces for the blaze."[*]

[*] Barrows Mussey, *We Were New England.*

The fireplaces were so high and so broad that there was a space at the side for a settle, which was allotted to the children. The custom of building a small window at the back was common in England, and when window panes of glass were available in the new country, an occasional fireplace had such a window at the back. The flames of the fire could be seen by all who passed, and this was a friendly gesture of welcome. Hospitality was the keynote of living in the old days. It has been said that in the South every home was like a tavern and every master was the host, so ready were the people to welcome and serve all who would enter and tarry.

Aside from the fireplaces of field stones or brick, there appear to have been some that were built of huge granite slabs — this, of course, in sections where granite abounded. The sides, floor and back were built of shaped slabs, the sides "beveling outward, a third slab on top and a deep fire-space sloping inward leading up the chimney throat." These slabs were obtained from quarries, and "when artisans of that period lacked the necessary blasting powder to separate the granite from the parent ledges, they filled the drill-holes with water and allowed the water to freeze. This procedure cracked the rock into required slabs."*

High-back settles stood at either side of the hearth — high, to keep the drafts from chilling those seated there. A wooden crane was often hung at one side of the fireplace to hold a

* From the writings of Jason Almus Russell.

blanket that acted as a screen from the cold. One can hardly realize the cold temperatures that had to be endured, but it has been written that ink froze in inkstands, and sap oozing from the burning logs froze before it caught fire.*

The opening of the chimney was so large that storms beat down and birds were often driven down to find shelter from the wind and cold. When one looks up into the throat of a huge chimney and sees the large patch of sky, one can believe that Benjamin Franklin could not have been wrong when he said that all but one-sixth of the heat went up the chimney. Ledges were sometime made at different levels as the chimney tapered, and on these the first lug pole rested, which at first was of wood and later of iron. Swallows often made their nests here until driven out by the winter fires. Such a chimney is

* From the diaries of Cotton Mather and Judge Samuel Sewall.

Big flat stones extending from the surface of the chimney base helped support the hearthstone above.

Niches made in chimney base provided excellent storage places for wine bottles.

seen in Buckman Tavern in Lexington, Massachusetts, built in 1690 (see page 63).

An early law provided that the chimney must be swept out every month, or the owner was fined for negligence. Thus the chimney-sweeps came into being, and from records of the time we learn that they had a very hard, mean job, with much risk and little compensation. It was only small boys who could go down the chimney, and with ropes around their waists they clung to the ledges as they worked, often falling and crippling themselves. On occasions they even refused to come out, trying to hide from their abusive and cruel masters.

Some chimneys had more than one flue, there being one for each of the several fireplaces, thus giving a direct draft for each fireplace. In one old house where there is a flue for each opening, the force of the draft was proved when one of the fireplaces was reopened after being sealed many years, and the draft in the room was so strong that the fireplace had to be sealed once more. Quite unlike this was the chimney with one central flue, which had to have a vent made in the attic because there was not enough draft for the several openings. Many and various were the ways and means of regulating flues and fireplaces, both in the earliest times and in the later changes.

Altering the size of the fireplace was not unusual; the fact that less wood was available seemed to be the principal reason for doing so. In the Simon Willard house, the original fireplace in the original one-room-and-loft house was approximately ten feet long. A second construction of brick brought the fireplace down to a smaller size; and a third was made by a later generation and an ornamental wooden mantel placed above, the room then being used as a ladies' chamber or sitting room. In the room on the opposite side of the entry (see page 30), the fireplace can doubtless boast of as many changes as ever came to any fireplace. It is said that seven times it was made smaller, thus having had eight different sizes. Now, in its present condition, it has its original back, with oven built into the chimney, and it has side walls left

from the first of the seven changes. At the time when marble mantel pieces were popular, the mistress of the house wished to be fashionable and she had the fireplace plastered over and papered and a mantel of marble set above. This was taken down by the present owner, of the ninth generation, and the room restored.

An odd arrangement, which was carried out during the time of one of the early generations, was an archway made in the left side wall of the fireplace so that the bake oven in the large fireplace in the adjoining room could be used (see page 30). Thus the bake oven served two fireplaces at right angles to each other, a thrifty New England arrangement. This large fireplace with its bake oven was never changed from its original size; it was in the lean-to of the four-room house, now used as a dining room since the final alteration of the house.

The first fireplaces had no ovens, all cooking being done in and over the fire. Later, the oven was built in the chimney at the back or at one side. This did not prove too popular, and soon the oven was built as a separate unit beside the chimney piece. Perhaps reaching over the fire was too difficult for the women folk and they conceived the idea of a change in the position of the oven.

The bake oven was constructed with an opening flush with that of the fireplace, at the height of about three feet, and with a deep sill. The foundation of the oven was square, often of stone, as some ruins show, with the exterior of brick. Many ovens were built entirely of field stones, but if bricks could be had it took less time to build with bricks. The oven was a bee-hive shape, with round floor and dome top, allowing the heat to rotate more readily, a principle learned from primitive people, who built their huts, adobes and igloos in this manner.

The early ovens were about thirty inches in diameter, and had an arched door with a wide threshold. Perhaps the dome-shaped top of loaves of bread gave the housewife the idea of an arched door to the oven. A door cover of wood was set close against the bricks and rested on a wooden handle, somewhat like a flatiron standing up and resting on its handle. Inside the opening at the top of the arch of the oven door was a small flue leading to the main chimney, which made a circulation of air within the oven and helped the wood to burn when the oven was being heated for baking. The bricks were so thoroughly heated that they held the heat for many, many hours.

The first ovens at the back of the chimney had no opening for a draft. After the wood was put in to make a fire for heating the oven, the wooden door cover was left open a crack to make a draft for the fire to draw. When a flue was built in the side bake ovens, near the opening, the fire burned toward the door and up the flue. After 1775, a flue was put in the top of the oven and it was then that iron doors were hung with slides in them, which allowed for drafts. Another type of ventilation was that which provided a vent in the floor of the bake oven, leading to the ash oven below; in this type the fire was built in the ash oven and the heat went through the vent to the bake oven above. This

was a direct way of heating but was an inferior arrangement, for the oven cooled off rapidly because the bricks were not so thoroughly heated.

Tin doors for the bake oven came when tin became obtainable, and by the beginning of the nineteenth century cast-iron doors swung on iron hinges, set on the outside edge of the threshold. The wooden door or the tin door was often used with the iron door, making two doors, which held the heat better than one.

In the Fairbanks House in Dedham, no oven was built in the original chimney, all cooking being done in the big kettles and pots over the fire. This house, which has been called the oldest house in the United States, has remained almost unchanged, never having been remodeled, and eight generations having made their home there up to 1903. In 1708, sixty-eight years after the house was built, a bake oven was put in at one side, at the time when such arrangements were proving more popular than an oven in the chimney, back of the fire. The top of the bake oven shows in the fireplace in the lean-to, which was added to the original house as an extra workroom.

An unusual arrangement of side ovens is

THIS KITCHEN IN THE ORIGINAL PART OF THE WAY-SIDE INN DISPLAYS FURNISHINGS AS THEY MUST HAVE LOOKED IN COLONIAL TIMES. *Maynard Workshop.*

The Manse at Old Deerfield boasts this grand ten-foot fireplace. Note oven at back and built-in cupboard at left.

the one in a house at Gill, Massachusetts, near Greenfield. The date of the house is 1736. Here there are three openings. The upper one is the bake oven, round, with dome-shaped top and wide threshold. The lower one is the ash oven, such as was found in many fireplaces of this period. The middle indentation is merely a deep threshold with a brick wall behind. In this, food was placed to be kept warm until used.

The ash oven, often found below the bake oven, was oblong in shape, with a square opening. The door cover of the ash oven went through the same process of changing from wood to tin to cast iron, as did the door of the bake oven.

Ashes were important because of the lye they contained, which was used in the spring batch of soap, the making of which is explained in Chapter Four. Ashes were left to accumulate on the hearth to help the fire burn better, but there was always an extra amount, and the ash oven helped out too. Each time the oven was heated for baking, by burning wood within the

oven itself, the ashes were removed and put into the ash oven or fireplace. In an old house in Northfield, Massachusetts, built in the early eighteenth century, there is a trap door in front of the hearth, down which the ashes were dropped into the cellar.

As the forests were depleted and wood became less plentiful, the fireplaces were built smaller in size. This brought the bake ovens down to a smaller size, and the shape was oblong instead of the first dome shape. There is no explanation for this change except that the oblong oven was simpler to make. Families became smaller when married children went to homes of their own instead of living under the same roof, as in the early years of the settlements, and this meant less baking in each home, with less need of huge ovens.

The central square chimney structure had but three fireplaces on the first floor, for the entry and staircase took one side. The large fireplace for the kitchen might be placed either directly back of the entry or at either side, for the location of the kitchen had to be such that the back door led directly to the yard and to the outbuildings and barn. The second and third fireplaces were small and shallow, the two side rooms being living room and bedroom, or, in later years, a dining room and a living room. These smaller fireplaces were used only to heat the rooms and never for cooking. But in the early four-room house, a second fireplace ad-

This early fireplace looks exactly as it did in colonial days except that the door is missing from the oven in the back.

(*Above*) TOP OF BAKE OVEN AND CHIMNEY CAN BE SEEN THROUGH THIS OPENING IN A ROOM ADJOINING THE KITCHEN. (*Right*) THIS UNUSUAL FIREPLACE HAS THREE INDENTATIONS AT THE RIGHT. UPPER ONE WAS A BAKE OVEN, MIDDLE WAS A FOOD WARMER, AND BOTTOM WAS AN ASH OVEN.

joining that of the kitchen was large to care for the extra work of making soap or dipping candles, dyeing or making apple butter.

Above the first-floor fireplaces, the chimney tapered perceptibly for the size of the chamber fireplaces above. This slope, called the shoulder, was used for closets made of pine paneling. The shelves were narrow, but made a convenient place for the toddy cup and for salt that had to be kept dry.

Upstairs there were three openings in the chimney, the staircase taking the fourth side, and the fireplaces here were made small and shallow. Sometimes in houses built at a later date, when heat was provided by stoves with stove pipes, the upstairs fireplaces were sealed and only the chimney was used. A mantel of wood, matching the woodwork of the room, was built above the sealed-up fireplace.

The chimney continued up into the attic or loft, then tapered to the size of the outside shaft, although many shafts were the size of the attic chimney. The first "catted" chimney was of wood, but after 1631, the chimneys were of stone or brick. Mortar was first made by mixing clay found in the soil with sand and crushed sea

shells or oyster shells, in lieu of lime. By 1638, lime was being imported in the South on whaling vessels which were carrying bricks from Jamestown, Virginia, in exchange. It was several years before New England or points west had lime.

Somewhere in the chimney structure—apparently anywhere from the base up—a smoke oven was made with a chimney flue. In this space, where fire could be laid for smoking meats, hooks were fastened into the ceiling, or poles were laid on the ledges. The fire was made from corncobs and hickory bark, which smudged with no flame, and each day a fresh fire was laid, taking three days to smoke the meat.

USUAL FIREPLACE ARRANGEMENT HAD BAKE OVEN ABOVE, ASH OVEN BELOW, AND OAK LINTEL AT THE TOP OF THE FIRE OPENING.

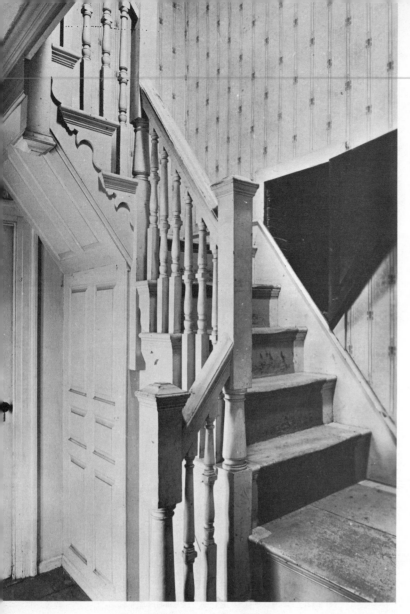

THE OPENING TO THE FOUR-FOOT SQUARE SMOKE ROOM OF THE SIMONDS TAVERN IN LEXINGTON, MASSACHUSETTS, IS INGENIOUSLY LOCATED ON THE STAIRWAY. *Lexington Historical Society.*

The first smoke oven, in the one-room or two-room house, was set into the chimney at the side of the fireplace. It was called a chimney oven. When cellars were built, the oven was placed in the chimney by the stairway leading down cellar. Other places for the oven were on the stairway going upstairs, on the landing, in "my lady's chamber," on the second floor, and even up in the attic. Sometimes, when the oven was upstairs, a separate opening was made on a lower floor or stairway or landing, in which the fire was built. If there was this second opening,

the meat was hung in the oven above and the door fastened; then the fire below could be attended to without disturbing the meat. When the smoke oven was so large that one stepped inside to hang the meat, or a whole animal, it was called a smoke room or a ham room.

Smoke houses, made of brick and looking much like large dog kennels, are sometimes seen in yards. They had two doors, one below for the fire and one above. The meat was placed on hooks or poles which were laid on irons driven into the brick walls. Or one large door might suffice. Sometimes the smoke house was built in the attic, against the chimney, doing away with the need of going outdoors to smoke the meat. Some of these inside structures were wooden frames, with a lining of paper smeared with tar.

In the William Hartwell house on the edge of Concord, Massachusetts, there is a large opening on the cellar stairway, directly back of the front-room fireplace. This is the size of a small room, and was called the smoke room or ham room.

In the Ralph Houghton house in Harvard, Massachusetts, there are two openings in the chimney against the stairway, on the landing. One oven has a square door and one has a larger, oblong door, both of them wooden. The smaller oven was for slabs of meat from the hog, while the larger one was for whole pigs. The larger opening was reached by a ladder; and carrying a dressed pig up the stairs and placing it on the hooks in the oven was a real feat of strength.

This chimney in the Houghton house, built in the late seventeenth century, is noteworthy for its structure. The base in the cellar is arched, the arch being a little less than six feet high at the keystone, five feet wide and fifteen feet deep. It is built of brick, with two-inch slabs of wood set in every two feet for supports; the keystone, running the entire length, is also of wood. On the inside of the arch are indentations for shelves, showing that the archway passage was used as a preserve closet or wine closet, although no trace of any door at the entrance is evident. The back end of the arch lies against solid earth.

further strengthened by the fact that the room added across the entry is of larger proportions, with windows farther apart than those of the first room, and the front door is not in the middle of the house. Historians call this an irregular house.

On the first floor, there are four fireplaces because of the irregular shape of the chimney, one at each end and one in each slanted side. The front entry and the stairway take up the long side, but the unusual three-sided extension of the chimney made the fourth fireplace possible. The largest fireplace and the bake oven are in the flat side of the chimney, in the original old kitchen; and a second large fireplace and bake oven are in one of the slanting sides, with

THE HORIZONTAL POLE FROM WHICH WHOLE ANIMALS WERE HUNG FOR SMOKING CAN BE SEEN AT UPPER RIGHT IN THIS INTERIOR VIEW OF THE SMOKE ROOM. A VENT FROM THIS ROOM CONNECTED WITH MAIN FLUE OF CHIMNEY.

THE SMOKE ROOM OR HAM ROOM OF THE HARTWELL FARM, LINCOLN, MASSACHUSETTS, IS LOCATED UNDER THE BASEMENT STAIRWAY AND ABOVE THE CHIMNEY FOUNDATION ARCHWAY.

One side of the base was built straight up to the floor above, while the other side was extended in a three-sided shape. In each of the three walls of the addition, there is an indentation, about eight inches deep, used for wine bottles.

At the top of the chimney structure in the cellar, huge flat stones were set in, extending two feet or more, giving support to the floor above and to the chimney as it continues. This way of topping the chimney structure in the cellar, mentioned earlier, was not uncommon.

The fact that at the back the chimney was laid against the solid earth leads to the conjecture that the original house had no cellar, being only a one-room house and loft. This theory is

57

smaller fireplaces in the other two sides. In the chambers above are four fireplaces, smaller and shallow.

On the upstairs landing are the two smoke ovens mentioned earlier. The doors are paneled to match the pine paneling of the entry and they were never set with hinges. Each was held with one button, and in taking the doors out, sharp tools have worn off the corners. The smaller door shows much taking-out, having been used more than the larger.

The smaller oven has a cavity three feet square and six feet deep. The roof of it slants to the chimney flue, which is a narrow slot about six inches wide and a foot in length. Poles on which the hams were hung reach from ledge to ledge; and a few nails are still there, which held the slabs of meat for smoking. On the floor of the cavity sits an iron kettle, in which corncobs and hickory bark were burned. There is no way of telling how old the kettle is or how long it has served. It had to be taken out with a long pole and hook, filled and put down in again. Gazing into the dark cavity and at the kettle on the bottom makes one realize something of the hard,

THIS OUTSIDE SMOKEHOUSE MADE OF BRICK WAS SET SOME DISTANCE AWAY FROM THE MAIN HOUSE AT THE OLD HADLEY FARM MUSEUM.

disagreeable labor which was mere routine work for our ancestors.

The second door opens into the larger smoke oven, which has the same flue as the smaller one. This door shows little sign of wear.

Another unusual feature of this chimney is the fact that each fireplace has a separate flue, straight up to the top of the chimney shaft. And the two smoke ovens enter into one flue, making nine flues to be seen at the chimney top. It is a massive, squatty chimney, sitting astride the roof of the old two-story house. Such a chimney structure from the base up called for expert builders, and one wonders how many chimneys exist that have so many sections as this one. Separate flues were built in houses of later periods, showing in the chimney shaft; such chimneys were known as pilastered chimneys.

The Houghton house was used as a garrison house and had four portholes in the four-room and lean-to structure. Here the neighbors gathered when fearful of an attack by the Indians. Generations later, when some repair work was being done in an upstairs bedroom, a loose brick was found at the side of the fireplace. Behind this was a till used by the early inhabitants for money or other valuables.

It is not uncommon to find the smoke oven in an upstairs bedroom or chamber. When such an oven was discovered and unsealed in Durham, New Hampshire, hams were found hanging where they had been left many years before. In another home, a small smoke oven in an upper chamber was never recognized as such by the later owners of the house, but was called a closet. In it were corncobs and ashes, relics of smoking meat long years ago, but explained by the owners, who knew nothing of smoke ovens, as having been brought in by squirrels.

In the Fairbanks house a smoke oven in the ladies' chamber was sealed by someone of a later generation who did not wish to have it there. One such chamber smoke oven exists in the old tavern in Northfield, Massachusetts, and it is occasionally used.

Sealing iron utensils in fireplaces and ovens that were closed for one reason and another was

STAIRWAY OPENINGS OF SMOKE OVENS IN THE RALPH HOUGHTON HOUSE, HARVARD, MASSACHUSETTS, WERE READILY AVAILABLE TO MEMBERS OF THE FAMILY.

(*Below*) EXTERIOR VIEW OF HOUGHTON HOUSE SHOWING LARGE CENTRAL CHIMNEY.

not an uncommon thing. So when an old fireplace is restored, or an oven is opened up, many an old kettle, pot or frying pan is brought to light.

By the beginning of the nineteenth century an addition to the chimney was built at the back of the house for a set kettle, or in the vernacular of the old folks, a "sit kittle." The structure was square and made of bricks, with a large brass kettle built in, coming flush to the top. Below this was a place for the fire, with an iron door with slides to make the draft. This set kettle was used when washing clothes. In some old houses a second built-in brick structure was made in which mash for the animals was cooked.

These kettles were made differently from

THIS KIND OF A BRICK STOVE WAS CALLED A SET
KETTLE BY OUR FOREFATHERS. THE KETTLE ON THE
LEFT WAS USED FOR BOILING CLOTHES WHILE THE
ONE ON THE RIGHT HELD HOT WATER TO BE USED IN
ANY ONE OF A MULTITUDE OF HOUSEHOLD ACTIVITIES.

those that hung over the fire for cooking, in that the band at the top edge was applied and riveted on, instead of the edge being rolled over an iron hoop. Thus they had a less finished look. Such kettles have frequently been sold at auctions in recent years, for the old washing arrangements have been dismantled for modern equipment.

A separate washhouse was common in Pennsylvania and in the South, with huge copper kettles built into the structure. The Shakers had a similar brick frame for their copper kettles used in making apple butter. The washhouse kettle could be scoured with vinegar and salt and used in making the apple butter.

The hearth or hearthstone was the floor of the fireplace on which the fire was built. The word hearth comes from various old words meaning coals, embers or "to burn." The first hearths were huge flat stones, such as were used also for doorsteps. The land abounded with rock of this sort, and the slabs taken for the hearthstone measured from twelve to fourteen feet long and six to eight feet wide. Bricks were used when they could be obtained, and many times were made use of in combination with the

IN THE KITCHEN OF THE HANCOCK-CLARKE HOUSE, BUILT IN 1698 AT LEXINGTON, MASSACHUSETTS, CAN BE SEEN A NUMBER OF EARLY HOUSEHOLD UTENSILS SUCH AS A MECHANICAL SPIT, BUTTER SCALES, SETTLE AND A CUPBOARD. *Lexington Historical Society.*

stone, the bricks forming the floor of the fireplace itself and the stone set in front.

Above the fireplace was the lintel, which is "a support that carries the weight of an opening, such as placed in doors, windows and fireplaces." That in the fireplace supported the weight of the chimney above. It was either a slab of rock or a huge squared log of oak, measuring as much as a foot in width and ten or more feet in length. An iron bar was used at a later date. It was into the oak lintel that the prong of a betty lamp or that of a crusie was jabbed, while the light from the wick lying in the oil gave out

its feeble ray. Often a brick or two was taken out near the lintel to make a place for the toddy cup to rest and to be kept warm, ready to be used.

In the William Hartwell house, bricks were left out at the side of the chimney near the smoke-oven opening, making a shelf about six inches wide and four inches deep. And in the back of the huge fireplace in the adjoining room, in the chimney itself, is a similar shelf. One had to stoop to place a toddy cup there, but it was high enough from the flames so that no harm could come to it.

In the Buckman Tavern in Lexington there is a hole above the huge oak lintel, which has passed unnoticed as something that had happened in the course of time. But to one who is looking for just such places where bricks have been taken out, it is logical to think that once the small shelf held the wooden toddy cup when stagecoach drivers and tired travelers stopped there. In the large taproom, with a bar in one corner and a huge fireplace, they warmed themselves with toddy or various other hot mixtures before retiring to the cold chambers above.

Stagecoach drivers drove an allotted distance — not more than thirty miles — and then, a relay of other horses and a fresh driver met them. The new driver continued, while they went back over the same route with the returning coaches. The drivers were paid a certain sum, and given their lodging and their food at the inn, which in turn was paid by the company. It was considered a wonderful feat to drive four and six horses, and drivers were often of one family, each succeeding generation taking over the job.

In an old stone tavern in Chesterfield, New Hampshire, there are three small rooms on the third floor where stagecoach drivers slept. In each room is a bunk only a foot high, with solid sides, like a low platform built into the corner of the room. On the front side of the bunk is an opening where sheathing was left out, and into this space the driver thrust his boots as he lay himself down to sleep. Doubtless there was some sort of a mattress, perhaps of straw, and some bed coverings; records tell of the drivers wrapping themselves in comfortables or quilts, which were the extent of their bedding.

In some inns, the drivers slept on the floor of the taproom with feet toward the fireplace, where the fire burned all night. They were awakened at three in the morning and went on their way with their passengers, to make another allotted number of miles. Boston stagecoaches left Boston at 3 A.M. and arrived at South Sudbury at Howe's Tavern (The Wayside Inn) about eight o'clock, in time for breakfast. For it was the custom to begin the journey long before daybreak and to have breakfast some hours later, at the first stop. This made a cold, bleak journey in the dark; as one passenger wrote, it was too dark to see that there were six horses, until daybreak showed up the two in front.

Shown in the illustration on this page is a carriage foot-warmer of tin used when traveling. A drawer slides out that held a long cake of charcoal, which was burned in the embers of the fireplace before being placed in the warmer. There is a vent which has a swivel protection used to create a draft to make the charcoal burn more rapidly and give greater heat. These foot-warmers were covered with ingrain carpeting.

The kitchen came in for its share of decoration when paneling was used; this was placed over the fireplace and at one side. Cupboards were built into the space above the lintel, and this was the ideal place for the toddy cups and mugs, which were first of wood and later of earthenware and glass. Salt, too, was kept in these cupboards. The paneling at the side of the fireplace served as a door for the bake oven; sometimes there were both an upper door and a lower door. This paneling gave a finished look

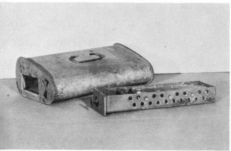

(*Far left*) TAVERN KEEPERS ACCOMMODATED THEIR GUESTS BY SUPPLYING THEM WITH WARM WATER CARRIED IN THIS KIND OF A TALL TIN PITCHER. THE ONE SHOWN HERE WAS PAINTED A BRIGHT PUMPKIN YELLOW. (*Left*) IN OLDEN TIMES, FOOT WARMERS WERE OFTEN CARRIED BY TRAVELERS.

THE FAMOUS BUCKMAN TAVERN IN LEXINGTON, MASSACHUSETTS, AND ITS TAPROOM WHERE THE CO-LONIAL MILITIAMEN MADE THEMSELVES COMFORT-ABLE THE NIGHT OF PAUL REVERE'S RIDE AND FROM WHICH THEY SALLIED FORTH IN THE MORNING TO MEET THE BRITISH REGULARS ON LEXINGTON GREEN.

to the kitchen. No doubt later generations added these improvements when they became the vogue, just as changes in styles of dress and manner of living came about.

The research worker may never know the original construction of some of these fireplaces and ovens, but can only figure from logical deductions how and when changes were made. By tapping walls around the chimney, oven doors can be located under plastering and paper, and many original constructions can thus be brought to light. Often plaster was added to the walls before the papering was done; all this can be taken off and the pine paneling exposed, which can then be cleaned and rubbed down. Many times fireplaces have been not only sealed but made smaller by additional walls of bricks, which can be taken down. One can study ceilings and floor boards to learn where entrances to a loft once held a ladder; where partitions of a room were torn out; or where walls were cut to make doors and windows. Smoke ovens are often found in hallways and on landings, sealed and papered over. Tapping will bring out a hollow sound where the wooden door is located.

Within the old fireplace were the andirons. These first came from the old country, but later were made by the village blacksmith. The andirons served two purposes: one was to hold the log, and the other to hold the spit on which the meat was roasted. This was a long, slender, pointed rod of iron.

The old name for andiron was "dog" or "firedog," from the idea that the head and the long body with feet suggested a dog; the two firedogs acted as guardians of the hearth. Many shapes were made, as the fancy of the smith directed. The ones made to hold the spit were called "spitdogs." One such set had a curved end at the top, through which the spit was thrust; sometimes the curve was frontward and sometimes backward. Others have broad brackets at the back on which the iron spit rested; there were several brackets at different heights so that the spit might be lowered or raised from the fire. Firedogs date from 1350 in England, and were cast in the beginning of the fifteenth century. Andirons are early mentioned as being something that held the spit.

An andiron with a knob at the top was called a cobiron — probably from this knob-shaped top, or cob. And to add variety, some andirons curve like a bird's long neck, hence the name gooseneck. Key andirons have a top shaped like a key handle. All such names show imagination and the association of ideas.

An elaborate pair of iron andirons which appear to be English have many additions for comfort. At the top of each andiron is a cup holder called a cresset. It was used to hold the basting cup while the meat roasted on the spit or held the toddy cup as it warmed in front of the fire. Some theories hold that the cup was also a place for a small pine knot for extra light when the fire was low. At the bottom of the andirons is a rod on which one could rest his feet and warm them as he imbibed his pleasing drink, hot and spicy. Above the floor rod was a place for another rod, which was the spit; this could be set at varying distances from the fire, and hooks suspended from it on which kettles could be hung. More simple forms of this elaborate pair were made by the colonial blacksmiths.

Brass andirons, too, were brought from across the water, having been common accessories of the fireplace in the old country. They were used in parlors and bedrooms in colonial times, and they are beautiful pieces of art; handed down from one generation to another, they are highly prized.

The earliest andirons, both of iron and brass, had a step-down in the flat bar that held the wood, which prevented the wood from coming out at the front; and a sliding bar was put

TWO FINE EXAMPLES OF OVEN DOOR PANELING THAT WERE BUILT AT THE SIDES OF FIRE-PLACES. NOTE HAND-WROUGHT HINGES AND EXCELLENCE OF CRAFTSMANSHIP IN PANELING SURROUNDING THE DOORS.

THIS FINE OLD FIREPLACE AND BAKE OVEN IN THE CELLAR OF WRIGHT'S TAVERN IN CONCORD, MASSACHUSETTS, WAS USED AS A BAKE SHOP IN THE EARLY DAYS.

THE COLONIAL LIGHTING EQUIPMENT SHOWN BELOW INCLUDES TINDER BOXES, THREE AND FOUR-WICK LAMPS MADE OF TIN AND, HANGING ABOVE, A MINER'S CANDLE HOLDER WHICH COULD BE HUNG UP OR STUCK IN THE WALL OF THE MINE. (*Below right*) THE TINDER BOW PRODUCED FIRE BY FRICTION WHEN USED WITH A CORD AND STICK.

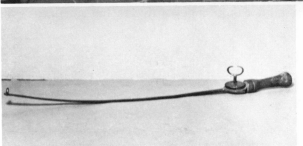

on to keep the wood from slipping off at the back. Later types of brass andirons had no step-downs, but instead had a brass ball a few inches from the upright standard, matching the ball of the upright. This prevented the wood from sliding toward the front.

The poker was the first of the fire tools, and two pokers used together made the first tongs. These were used to carry coals as well as to poke the fire. Pokers, tongs and shovels make up the equipment for the fireplace, and were made of iron or of brass and iron. Large hooks, called jamb hooks, were screwed into the bricks to hold the iron sets, and elaborate standards of brass were created to hold the sets of brass.

Artists have portrayed the bringing in of the Yule log on a wooden sledge drawn by two men or a horse or even by two oxen, coming through the wide kitchen door, first called the hall door. It is a picturesque scene of festivity —

cold weather without, and warmth, cheer and holiday expectations within. Such pictures have given the modern generations an idea of the size of the logs for the fire, and the size of the openings of the fireplace, as well as an idea of the large andirons.

In those early days, when night came the fire was "raked," and covered with a curfew cover to keep it from going out. This cover, made of copper, was a large dome-shaped affair, filled with perforations to allow some air to reach the fire and keep the wood smoldering. The old French word for curfew was *courefeu*, meaning "to cover the fire"; this was the time of day when a bell was rung in the village as a signal to cover the fire and go to bed. With nothing but flint for striking sparks to light a fire, it was quite a task to make a new fire, and the early settlers prided themselves on the fact that they could keep the same fire throughout the year. The tinder box held the flint, striker and rags, and was kept on the shelf over the fireplace or in the cupboard above. If by misfortune the fire did go out, embers had to be borrowed from a neighbor, even though the neighbor might live a mile or more away. The embers were carried in a small tin box with a handle. A bride always took such a box with her from her old home for good luck and a blessing on the new home.

Sparks for fire have been created in tinder since time immemorial. The Indians and other savages used flint from the soil, or twirled a stick between their hands to cause enough friction to create fire. Illustrated is a tinder bow of iron. A cord was fastened in the eye at one end and wound around a key with a rachet turn near the handle. The cord was twisted around the middle of a small stick. The stick was pressed on a stone or a piece of metal, with tinder near it, and the bow was drawn back and forth, while the stick was held firmly as it was twirled. This caused friction and made a spark. Tinder wheels and other contrivances were also used, precursors of the many types of friction matches.

One kind of tinder box had on its cover a holder for a candle. Within was a small metal striker, a piece of flint, strips of rags and a small tin cover with a small ring handle. The striker was struck sharply against the flint, causing a spark which set fire to the rags; the candle was lit from the blaze and the small cover snuffed out the fire in the rags. Then the cover to the box was put on and the candle was ready to use.

AN INDIAN DEMONSTRATING THE EARLIEST METHOD OF PRODUCING FIRE BY FRICTION. THE EARLY SETTLERS ALSO STARTED THEIR FIRES IN THIS MANNER.

III

Antique Kitchenware and How It Was Used

IT WAS A meager array of cooking utensils that stood on the hearth in the homes of those early settlers. Brought to this country with them, along with whatever other possessions could be taken, these utensils represented the necessary equipment for preparing meals in the fireplace. They had probably already seen years of service before being brought to the new country. Iron, copper and brass were in the allotment which the passengers were allowed to bring with them, and there were pots, kettles, gridirons, frying pans, skillets, trivets and some odd utensils that had strange names.

Primitive man cooked over fire out in the open, and a fire hole was the earliest means of cooking. A small pit was dug in the ground and lined with stones. Then a fire was built in the pit. When the stones had become hot, the embers were taken out and a pot of meat was placed on the bottom of the pit, the hole was covered with skins on boughs and sealed as airtight as possible.

Food was also cooked in pots and kettles hung over an open fire, suspending from a pole held by two or more crotched poles driven into the ground a short distance apart. Sometimes two trees served to hold the pole for the kettle. Meat to roast was hung on cords over the embers.

The first fireplace of the colonies had a wooden lug pole on which hung pots and ket-tles; the pole rested on ledges, high up at the sides of the chimney throat. The word lug means an ear or projection, such as a ledge. The lug pole was also called a trammel-bar, because it held the trammels or pot-hooks. Many a dinner was lost when the pole became charred from the heat and let the kettles down into the embers. In 1720, an iron crane was conceived, a Yankee invention, and this was fastened to the side wall of the fireplace, swinging out over the hearthstone.

The history of iron covers many chapters, but the interest of a main chapter centers in America in 1646, when the first models and castings were made for domestic implements and iron tools, by Joseph Jenks of Lynn. The first iron foundry in America had been erected at Lynn in 1643, by John Winthrop, Jr., but it was not for another three years that molds were made.

The first pot to be cast is now in the possession of the direct descendants of Thomas Hudson, first owner of the Saugus River land, living in Lynn. The pot weighs two pounds and thirteen ounces; holds one quart, less one gill; and measures four and a half inches in diameter on the inside, and four and a half inches deep. The first cast-iron teakettle was made about 1760, the ones before that date having been wrought iron and imported from England. The first copper teakettle was used at Plymouth in

1702. In 1748, New York and Connecticut were shipping iron to England, and by 1750 the iron industry had become secure.

In those days there was always a blacksmith, who worked on a forge on castings; a whitesmith, also called a tinsmith, who worked on tin, and finished or polished iron castings; and a silversmith, who worked with silver and other fine metals. These men were held in high esteem because of their important contributions to society, and in olden times they sat as honored guests at banquets and were ranked before physicians. In time of war they were sometimes captured by the enemy to prevent further weapons from being made.*

The cast-iron kitchen utensils such as pots, pans and skillets were called "hollow ware." The making of them began in 1725, although not in large numbers; few were listed in wills. "Sad ware" was the flat ware, such as plates.

Pots and kettles, as mentioned earlier, hung from the lug pole or crane. It is interesting to note that there was a distinction between a pot

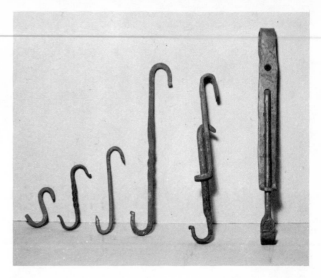

THESE ANTIQUE POT HOOKS AND TRAMMELS HANDED DOWN FROM EARLIER TIMES HAVE UNDERGONE LONG YEARS OF HARD USE.

A VERY OLD CAST-IRON POT WITH A HOLE IN IT FROM WHICH THE STEAM ESCAPES. ONE FOOT HAS BEEN BURNED OFF FROM LONG USE.

and a kettle. A pot had bulging sides and a cover, while a kettle had sloping sides and no cover of its own. This distinction in the use of these words is not always made today.

There was always a supply of hot water swinging on the crane, not only for cooking, but for soap-making, candle dipping or cheese-making, or for dyeing. Families prided themselves in having many brass kettles, regardless of whether the family was rich or poor, and those

* J. L. Bishop, *History of American Manufacturers.*

kettles were bright spots in the dark rooms. They were kept clean and shining, the task of polishing them being allotted to the daughters, whose training in learning to share the burdens of their parents began at an early age.

Some of the kettles were of great size, holding as much as fifteen gallons; these, called caldrons (or cauldrons), were of copper, brass or iron. At times they were valued as high as four hundred dollars, and a man was proud to leave in his will his kettles of copper and brass. The iron pots and kettles were held in little esteem in comparison with those of copper and brass, often being traded to the Indians in exchange for skins, fur and corn.

The hooks on which the pots and kettles hung were of two varieties: single ones from four to sixteen inches long; and the trammels or "hole-and-peg" hooks. These latter were two hooks set into each other in notches so that they might be lengthened or shortened, as the need arose. Some of them have an extension of six feet, the length needed in the first huge chimneys when the lug pole was set so high from the embers, up on the ledges of the chimney throat. There were pot chains, a combination of hooks and chains: a long arm with a hook at the end

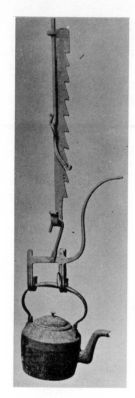

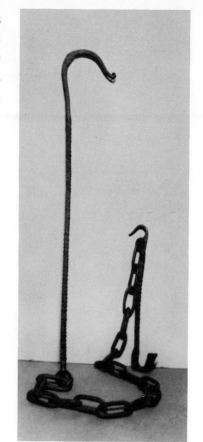

that hung on the lug pole, and hooked into this a long chain of heavy links, then another arm that set into the chain, and had a hook on the end of which hung the kettle. These pot chains were six or eight feet in length, and were made of heavy wrought iron.

Hooks were first mentioned in 1643 in the records of the estate of Abraham Belknap of Lynn. The plain hooks were called pot-hooks, chimney-hooks, hakes, pot-hangers, pot-claws, pot-clips, pot-brakes and pot-crooks, all names that came into use among the various village folk. Sometimes the shank of a hook was twisted to make for an artistic appearance.

There was a rachette pot-hook which was a contrivance for tipping the iron teakettles as they hung over the fire. This contrivance, a frame that hung on the crane and had two hooks on which the kettle swung, was called a "kettle-tilter," "idle-back" or "lazy-back." The frame measured about ten inches long, and a long handle extended at one side with which the kettle was tipped as the water or tea was needed. A lock prevented the kettle from tipping as it swung. A few of these kettle-tilters have survived to present time.

The pots and kettles that swung on the lug pole or crane had no feet, merely a round bottom. Those that stood on the hearth and in the embers had three short legs, raising them up from the embers but allowing them to be over the heat. A still later type appeared when stoves were made, and those had a projection which set into stove holes. The handles on iron pots and kettles were called "hoop handles"; the term bale handles was applied to those on wooden buckets and pails. Sometimes a pot or kettle had a half-hoop and a swivel ring, or a swivel ring on a whole hoop, by which it hung.

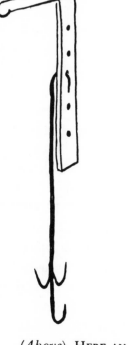

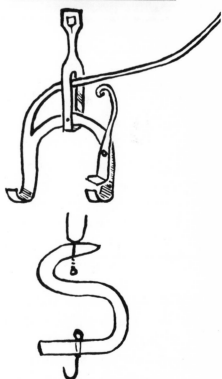

(*Above*) HERE AN ANCIENT IRON TEAKETTLE HANGS ON AN IDLE-BACK WHICH IN TURN IS SUSPENDED FROM A POTHOOK. *Gertrude Jekyll (Drawing)* MEATS WERE COOKED IN FRONT OF THE FIRE AFTER BEING MOUNTED ON THE ADJUSTABLE HOOK OF THIS DANGLE-SPIT.

(*Above*) HAND-WROUGHT AND HAND-FORGED CHAIN TRAMMEL WAS USUALLY HOOKED OVER THE LUG POLE IN THE CHIMNEY THROAT. (*Top drawing*) A KETTLE TILTER, BY WHICH A KETTLE WAS TIPPED WITHOUT REMOVING IT FROM THE FIREPLACE. OTHER DRAWING SHOWS A JACK RACK.

THESE INTERESTING OLD HAND-WROUGHT ANDIRONS OR FIRE-
DOGS WERE BROUGHT TO THE COLONIES FROM ENGLAND. NOTE
TODDY-CUP HOLDERS AT TOP OF ANDIRONS AND BRACKETS ON
UPRIGHTS FOR SPIT ROD TO HOLD ROASTING MEAT. *Gertrude
Jekyll.*

The most primitive method of roasting was done with the long, slender spit, which was thrust through the meat and placed before the fire. The first ones were of hazel wood and were whittled by hand; the later ones were of iron.

The simplest way of hanging a wooden spit was to fasten it in front of the fire by a cord. The cord was twisted, and as it untwisted by its own momentum, it turned all sides of the roast toward the fire. The task of keeping the cord twisted was left to the children. "Done to a turn" is an expression coming down to us from the time when the meat was turned on a spit in front of the fire. A drip pan or a skillet was placed beneath to catch the drippings.

The iron spit was set into the loop heads of the andirons, the spit andirons, that stood on the hearth. Or the andirons might have brackets at the back on which the spit was placed. These were turned by clock-jacks.

There was also a basket spit, which enclosed a joint of meat; rods extending at the ends of the basket rested on the bar of the andiron. Another type had two prongs that held the meat. At one end of such spits was a wheel, around which a belt was secured, connected with a clock-jack. These first appeared in Europe in the sixteenth century.

Two inventions from the old country were the dangle-spits and the jack racks. The dangle-spit was constructed like a trammel, with two parts that raised or lowered the meat to the heat. The lower part was an iron rod, at the end of which were three or four hooks onto

70

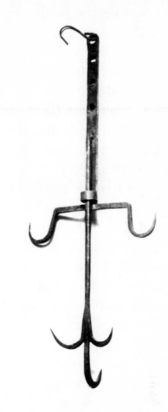

which the meat was caught, and the upper part hung on the crane by a chain and hook. More than one piece of meat could be hooked onto the dangle-spit.

The jack rack was an S-shaped iron that screwed onto the mantel shelf, with a second screw at the bottom that held a hook on which the meat was hung. The word "jack" seems to imply something that rendered assistance, and perhaps it was related to the custom of calling a boy or any attendant that helped by the name of Jack. The wooden bootjack helped take off boots, and the iron jack or kitchen jack held the meats before the fire.

Clock-jacks, made of brass and of iron, are elaborate arrangements of clock wheels, weights and chains. They were fastened to the wall above the fireplace and, by means of a cord, they turned the spit before the fire. Such a jack is fastened over the fireplace or on the mantel in a few old houses or taverns today. The Wayside Inn in Sudbury has a very beautiful one, an unusual one hangs in Wright's Tavern in Concord, another one in the Essex Museum in Salem and still another type, of iron, in the Rufus Putnam house on the outskirts of Worcester. The one in the Rufus Putnam house once screwed onto the wall by the fireplace and turned a huge iron cage which held the meat suspended in a frame standing high on four legs, the width of the fireplace opening.

An unusual contrivance for turning the spit was an iron fan, set up in the chimney flue,

(*Top Left*) THIS FISH ROASTER LOOKS LIKE A BREAD TOASTER EXCEPT FOR THE HOOKS ON WHICH FISH WERE SET TO COOK. (*Top right*) DANGLE-SPIT USED FOR COOKING MEAT OR FISH. HERE IT IS HUNG ON A JACK RACK. (*Middle*) AN OLD-FASHIONED BASKET SPIT FASTENED TO A SET OF ANDIRONS. (*Bottom*) THE SAME PAIR OF ANDIRONS SUPPORT AN OLD-TIME PRONGED ROASTING SPIT. *Gertrude Jekyll.*

71

which was kept in motion by the draft passing up the chimney. Chains extended to the spit in front of the fire, and the spit was turned by the revolving of the fan. Such a fan to turn the spit is found at Mount Vernon, and there is also one in the Wentworth-Gardner house in Portsmouth, New Hampshire. Doubtless some others are still in old chimneys, relics of this primitive way of cooking.

The strange custom of turning the spit by the power of a dog was begun in the old country, and for a short time was practiced in this country. A hole was made in the wall, high up at one side of the fireplace, and a cage with a wheel, not unlike a squirrel's cage and wheel, was set in the hole. The wheel was attached to a spit in front of the fire. A dog was shut in the cage, and as he turned the wheel it set in motion the spit which turned the meat. The dog was a small breed with a long body and short crooked legs; the name "turnspit" was given to him because of his use in the kitchen. It was surely not a pleasant thing for the dog, and sometimes the dog was reluctant to do his task; then live coals were placed in the cage to accelerate his speed. The meat might weigh two or three times as much as the dog, and it took three hours before it was done. It is said that the dogs knew when roasting day came, probably by the odor of the fresh meat as it was being prepared, and they went off and could not be found the entire day. Wise dogs!

By 1790, a tin roasting oven had been invented, and this proved very convenient and popular; occasionally it is used at the present time. Some sources give the date of this invention as 1729. It was a reflector oven, a half-cylinder in shape, and standing on four feet. At the back was a small door that lifted, through which the meat could be watched and basted. The bottom of the oven was curved to catch the juices, and at one end was a snout out of which the juices were poured when the meat was done. A spit ran through the oven, passing through a hole at one end and out a slot at the other end. The spit had a crank by which it was turned, and at the other end was a point that set into small holes on the side of the oven, to hold it in position. The meat was fastened to the spit with skewers, six or eight inches long, which fit into small slits in the spit, three or four skewers being used for a roast. When the meat was done, the spit, with the meat on it, was taken out by pulling up a rod at the end which opened the slot.

This sort of oven has been called a "tin kitchen" as well as a roasting oven; some dictionaries have called it a Dutch oven. But the Dutch oven is by all rights the iron kettle with cover, which appeared at a much earlier date.

There were many sizes of the tin kitchen, from those a foot in length to those of four feet, used in large fireplaces. They are seen today in old taverns and inns, as well as in homes where such primitive articles give the domestic atmosphere of the early life. At taverns and inns that have these ovens, guests sometimes call for their roast to be done in the tin kitchen, and the meat is especially enjoyed with the extra flavor of romance.

The skewers, wrought by hand on the anvil, are thin and sharp-pointed, with small eyelets by which they could be hung on the iron holders, six skewers making a set. The holder

OVER TWO DOZEN KITCHEN AND COOKING ACCESSORIES ARE SHOWN CLUSTERED AROUND THIS FIREPLACE. NOTE CLOCK JACK AT LEFT, BANNOCK BOARD ON SHELF, TRIVET, GRIDIRON, SKEWERS ON HOLDER, LADLES AND FRYING PAN. *Clayton Jenks.*

also was hand-wrought, with two arms and a handle by which it hung by the fire, ready to be used at all times. Everything was either hung or set on legs to make for greater orderliness.

Birds such as pigeons and bob-whites (quails) were roasted in smaller ovens, which were of iron as well as of tin. There are today some very rare hand-wrought iron holders which are about a foot square, a frame standing on legs, with a trough at the bottom of the frame. On the top bar are four or five hooks on which the birds were hung by their breasts, and as they cooked the juices ran down into the narrow trough below. The frame pivots on its base of four legs, and the birds could thus be turned about and roasted on all sides. Two such iron roasters are in the museum of Mr. A. B. Wells, of Southbridge, Massachusetts, who is now completing a village at Sturbridge, with dams, mill, store, church, tavern and homes around a common.

Tin kitchens for roasting birds are not as rare as those of iron, having come into use at a later date. One in existence today has two rows of hooks fastened to a flat back of tin about eight inches high and a foot in length with a base and a raised edge to catch the juices. There is a handle at the back on which the oven rested and by which it was carried. The tin reflected the heat as the roaster stood in front of the fire.

A rare roaster, also of tin, is the one for roasting apples. This, too, set on its handle in front of the fire and the two shelves held three or four apples each. The shelves were curved to hold the juice as it ran from the sizzling apples, toasting slowly before the great fire.

Still another rare roaster is the one of iron used for roasting rabbits. Instead of four legs, it has two brackets which allowed it to be turned on one side when it stood before the fire. Four strips of iron, with jagged edges, are fastened with rivets to the floor of the roaster, and on these the two dressed halves of the rabbit were hung. The edge of the roaster is turned up to catch the juices, acting as a drip pan. The frame measures a foot wide and fifteen inches long, and the standards are six inches high.

FRONT AND REAR VIEW OF A ROASTING KITCHEN SHOWING SPIT AND SKEWERS. THERE IS NO REASON WHY A SIMILAR CONTRIVANCE COULD NOT BE USED WITH PRESENT DAY FIREPLACES.

SKEWERS HUNG UP ON SKEWER HOLDERS. ALTHOUGH SKEWERS ARE ONLY OCCASIONALLY USED IN MODERN COOKERY, THEY WERE INDISPENSABLE IN PREPARING A ROAST IN OUR GREAT-GREAT-GRANDPARENTS' DAY.

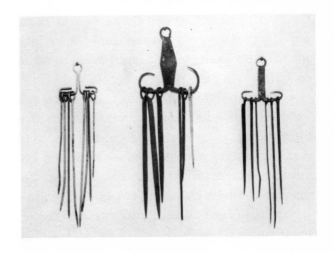

73

TWO DISTINCTIVE TYPES OF ROASTERS WERE IN COMMON USE IN COLONIAL TIMES, ONE FOR BIRDS AND THE OTHER FOR APPLES.

This rabbit roaster, as well as the apple roaster of tin, was found in a home that was broken up by the death of the last member. The apple roaster had been labeled by one of the third generation.

The Dutch oven, often called a fire-pan in early times, is another relic of the past. As explained earlier, the name Dutch oven has erroneously been given to the side bake oven in the fireplace and to the tin roasting kitchen. Correctly used, the term in the early colonies meant a shallow iron receptacle with three short legs and a loop handle. It measured about fifteen inches in diameter. The cover had a rim which held the embers heaped onto the kettle as it stood in the fireplace, thus carrying out the first principle of cooking in the fireplace before the brick oven was built at the side of the chimney. This Dutch oven was used for bread, which was called fire cake, and the oven could be taken on journeys if necessary.

Bread in the South was made into cakes and baked on the head of an iron hoe, with the handle sticking out in the room. Such cakes were made of Indian meal, or Indian meal and rye meal, and were called "hoe cakes," from the manner in which they were baked.

In the North, similar cakes were baked on small oblong boards of wood called bannock boards, and the cakes were called "bannock cakes" or bannock bread. The board was propped up against the kettles, or on its own handle if it happened to have one, the handle being of wood like the board. A few such boards are still to be found; but wooden ware was easily turned into kindling wood, and many interesting old pieces have thus been lost.

When the brick oven appeared, bread was baked in loaves, within the opening. In the oven itself a fire was built of maple or birch wood — sometimes of the slow-burning beech — and before the wood had burned to ashes, when the roof was "white hot," the embers were taken out and put into the fireplace or into the ash oven below. This was done with a long-handled iron peel called an ash peel, or slice. This ash peel was made by the village blacksmith, and there were as many different shapes as there were peels. Heads, shanks and the ends of the handle all differed; and on seeing a collection of them one senses the creative ability of the village smith.

THIS RABBIT ROASTER, LIKE MOST OTHER ROASTERS, WAS PLACED IN FRONT OF A HOT FIRE WHEN PREPARING THE FAMILY DINNER.

HERE IS A GOOD EXAMPLE OF A DUTCH OVEN, THE FIRST OVEN USED FOR BAKING. IT WAS SET INTO EMBERS WHICH WERE ALSO HEAPED ON THE COVER.

After the embers had been taken out and put into the bed of the fire or into the ash oven below the bake oven, the oven was swept clean with a birch broom, and oak leaves or cabbage leaves were placed on the oven floor to hold the loaves of bread, in lieu of a pan. A long-handled wooden shovel called a bread peel or slice was used to put the loaves into the oven.

The early shovels had heads of various shapes — square, round or "shovel-shaped" — with a thin edge, always much worn and showing signs of rubbing on the blackened bottom of the oven. The shovel was sprinkled with corn meal, the loaves put onto it and slid into the oven, and with a quick snap of the wrist the loaves slid off onto the leaves. In the same way, they were taken out when done. A bread peel was given to a bride as an omen of good luck for her new home. Similar shovels were used by bakers in early Roman times, and are still used in bakeries today.

An odd bread peel, supposedly from New Jersey, has been added to the author's museum. It has a round, iron head to which is welded a flat rim, and to this a socket handle about six inches long is joined. A wooden pole handle five feet long sets into this iron socket.

Tin reflector ovens, rectangular in shape, were used for baking biscuits. These ovens stood on legs and were flat on all sides, with one side open to the fire. A tin shelf at either side rested on a ledge. Some ovens were made in two sections, one part sitting in the other, and the upper part acting as a cover that was lifted when the biscuits were put in or taken out. Others were made in one piece. These ovens stood in front of the fire for the biscuit-baking. There are many sizes of biscuit ovens, ranging from a foot in length to more than two feet. The size perhaps depended on the size of the family.

A later biscuit oven of still different type, found in an old house, is oblong in shape. It has a shelf, and a door on hinges that opens from the top down. The back tapers to hold a thin iron pot ten inches deep and five inches in diameter, with a grating at the bottom. The pot, which has a handle by which it could be removed, was for charcoal, which was used when baking biscuits, and the oven could be moved about, using its own heat. It appears to be one of those one-of-a-kind utensils which occasionally happened, something made by a local smith at a particular request or as a new invention.

ON THIS WOODEN BANNOCK BOARD CAKES OF CORN MEAL, CALLED BANNOCK CAKES, WERE PLACED BEFORE THE FIRE TO BAKE.

Another type of a tin baking oven has two compartments, each with a door and a shelf. This oven is a yard long, and sets high on tin legs. At the back is a place for the fire pot, now missing. This was connected with the chimney, for there is a small stovepipe running from the fire pot. Such ovens were in use when charcoal was a common commodity in the homes.

An iron pot holding charcoal is a brazier, or brasier. This was used in cooking and also to keep food warm and as a means of warming a cold room. It has a grating in the top to hold the kettles, pots or dishes.

AT THE RIGHT ARE TWO LONG-HANDLED WOODEN SHOVELS CALLED BREAD PEELS OR SLICES WHICH WERE USED TO PLACE LOAVES OF BREAD INTO BRICK OVENS. AT THE LEFT STAND THREE IRON ASH PEELS USED FOR REMOVING EMBERS FROM THE BAKE OVEN.

THIS SINGULAR IRON BREAD PEEL, SAID TO HAVE COME FROM NEW JERSEY, HAS A ROUND IRON HEAD WELDED TO A FLAT RIM AND A FIVE-FOOT WOODEN POLE-HANDLE.

a small grating onto which the charcoal was placed; the ashes were taken out at the small opening in front.

Skillets are listed in the first records of articles brought from across the water. They are shallow, rounded iron pans on three legs, with a straight handle extending at the side. They vary in size from six inches in diameter to about a foot. In the early days they were called "posnets" or "pipkins," and were used when cooking in the embers. All iron utensils that were used in the embers were called "down-hearth" utensils.

Another form of the skillet is the iron pan that resembles a frying pan — shallow, and having straight sides and a flat bottom, instead of rounded. It has a short handle and three short legs, and was sometimes called a spider. The

one in the author's collection has a patch riveted to the side where the handle broke off and was made secure again — a sign of old-time thrift.

Frying pans, or "fry pans," were another necessary utensil of iron. In Leviticus, ii: 7, the mention of the frying pan shows that it was a common utensil: "And if thy oblation be a meat offering baken in the frying pan, it shall be made of fine flour with oil." The handles of the frying pan were fully three feet in length so that the housewife might stand back from the fire as she cooked her meal. At the tip of the handle was a hole by which the pan was hung by the fire when not in use. A sign of thrift is shown again in the pan in the author's collection — a large patch riveted to the front edge where the greatest wear came. These old iron utensils that survived centuries of hard usage might have many a tale to tell of life in earlier days.

The short-handled frying pan came into use when stoves became common. They are made in different sizes and numbered accordingly. But these later utensils do not have the sturdy appearance of their forebears.

In the author's collection there is a double

boiler of iron, and this kind of utensil was probably the first used on a stove. A pot with straight sides sits in a larger pot with bulging sides, allowing the water to circulate around the inside pot. Each pot has a handle, showing that either could be used separately. These pots were perhaps used on a crane over a fire.

An important piece of the equipment for the fireplace which came from the old country was the trivet, dubbed the "footman." This was a stand with three long legs and tiny feet, and a top of either iron or brass. The tops were made in various shapes, round, square, oblong, ellipti-

THIS LONG TIN BAKING OVEN, FUELED BY CHARCOAL, CONSISTS OF TWO COMPARTMENTS, EACH WITH A DOOR AND A SHELF, AND A FIRE POT AT BACK CONNECTED WITH THE CHIMNEY. EQUIPPED WITH HANDLES AT EITHER END, IT COULD EASILY BE CARRIED ABOUT.

cal or shaped to follow a design. Many in existence today have beautiful patterns, and an old trivet is an ornament to any fireplace. They were used to hold kettles or dishes of food or even as plate warmers, standing on the hearth before the fire.

The "cat," a variation of the trivet, is an odd creation that appeared with the trivet in 1692. It was made of wood or iron, and was really three sticks crossed in the middle, making a crotch to hold a dish. Whichever way it stood, three arms extended upward, three legs downward. Like a cat, it always came to rest securely on its legs, no matter which way it was turned.

The first gridiron, made of wood, was a grating or rack on legs, with a handle. These were used for broiling fish or meat. The early ones had long legs, but in due course of time gridirons were made with shorter legs, which in later years were not more than three inches long. After those of wood, came those of wire, and it is said that George Washington had one of that type. The iron gridirons came in at the time when iron was used for fireplace utensils.

(*Left, top to bottom*) THIS BRAZIER HEATED FOOD AND WARMED A COLD ROOM. THE FIRST UTENSIL TO BE USED ON THE STOVE WAS PROBABLY THE DOUBLE BOILER OF IRON. REFLECTOR OVENS WERE PLACED ON THE HEARTH FOR BAKING BISCUITS. THE FRY PAN WITH ITS THREE-FOOT HANDLE ENABLED THE HOUSEWIFE TO REACH INTO THE HUGE FIREPLACE. THE SHORT-HANDLED PAN CAME INTO USE WITH THE ADVENT OF STOVES. (*Right, top to bottom*) A TRIVET FOR THE HEARTH AND TWO SKILLETS FOR COOKING IN THE EMBERS.

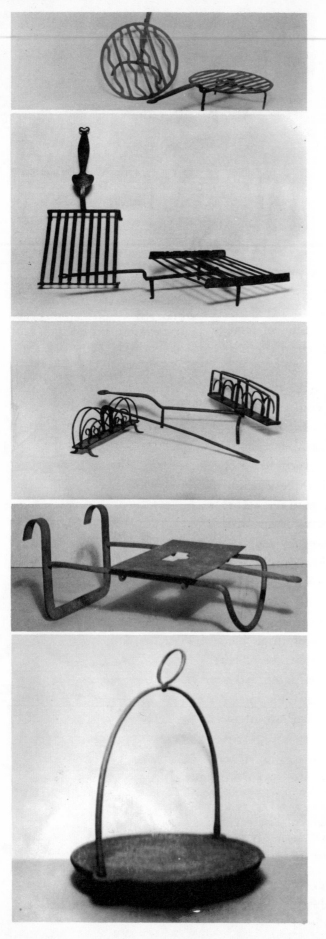

The head was round or square, pivoting on a center pin held by a three-legged stand with an extending handle. Some of the square-headed gridirons had built-up sides to hold the food from slipping over the edge. Gridirons with a square head and four short legs were of a later period, and they were often made with grooved slats. Drip pans were placed underneath in the embers to catch the juices of the meat; one such made of tin and having a handle was not unlike a dustpan in appearance.

A sausage-baker, on which the sausages were baked on bent wires in a holder, may have been like the tin bird roaster; or perhaps in some localities a different oven was fashioned for this purpose. There was, however, scarcely any utensil that was not adaptable to other purposes than that for which it was made.

Iron plate warmers were hung on a cross bar between the andirons, or rested on the hearth. An unusual one in the author's collection has a plate of copper, which slides to adjust according to the size of the plate that rested on it. When tin for utensils became obtainable and popular, a tin plate warmer was made in the shape of shelves on legs, solid back and open front. This faced the fire, and a door at the back made it possible to put in or take out the plates and dishes. These tall tin plate warmers were often painted like the tin trays, apple dishes and other articles then popular.

The griddle was another utensil of iron used in baking, originally called girdle, from the Scotch and provincial English. Like the griddle of today, it consisted of a flat, round plate

THE TWO TOP PHOTOGRAPHS AT THE LEFT SHOW SEVERAL DIFFERENT TYPES OF EARLY AMERICAN GRIDIRONS: A ROUND ONE WHICH IS PIVOTED, ANOTHER SQUARE AND STATIONARY, AND THE THIRD PIVOTED. THE CENTER PHOTOGRAPH IS OF TWO HAND-WROUGHT TOASTERS. THE ONE AT THE LEFT HAS A HINGED HANDLE, THE OTHER A FRAME THAT PIVOTS ON HANDLE. IN THE TWO LOWER PICTURES ARE SHOWN A PLATE WARMER OF COPPER WITH A SLIDING SHELF, AND A GRIDDLE WITH A HOOP HANDLE AND A SWIVEL SO THAT IT COULD BE HUNG ON A CRANE.

with a hoop handle, and it used to hang on the crane when oat cakes, or later, buckwheat cakes, were being baked. One type had a half-loop handle with a swivel ring. Some of these griddles were made with three short legs so that they could stand in the embers; these either had hoop handles and a swivel, or a projecting handle like a spider. Griddles which the Indians of Virginia used were made of stone or pottery. If the stone was soapstone, the griddle needed no greasing. The cakes were turned with a spatula of wood, tin or iron. Griddle cakes suggest the well-known story of King Alfred and the cakes, which has been told many times. King Alfred, who lived in the ninth century, was in hiding, and took shelter in the hut of a poor herdsman. Cakes were baking on the hearth and the herdsman's wife left the king to watch them. But, lost in thought, he paid no attention to them, until she returned and found them burning. Then she cried out: "You lazy good-for-nothing! You can't even be trusted to watch the cakes — though you are willing enough to eat them!" One wonders if these cakes were baked on something like a griddle.

Toasters, used for bread and possibly for cheese, were on the early hearths in many designs and types. They were hand-wrought, those of a later period had a wooden handle on a hinged arm. The wrought-iron designs are often very delicate, and these utensils were perhaps the most beautiful of the early iron equipment. In some toasters the head revolves and the handle is made in one piece with the base; while others have a jointed handle, and the head and base are in one piece. By such differences one can tell approximately the period of their production. Four small feet held the toaster up from the hearth.

A toaster or broiler for fish is little seen. It has a rack resting on four small feet. From the top bar, seven curved hooks with sharp ends extend downwards. A long handle is hinged to the top bar, by which the toaster was carried or turned about. The fish was thrust onto the hooks and either toasted or broiled as the implement stood in front of the fire. A fish could

have been placed within the curved hooks instead of being jabbed onto the hooks.

There is an iron trammel which held fish for broiling or roasting. This has three hooks at the end of one part and a cross bar with hooks on the other end. It hung on the crane and could be adjusted to the fire. Another broiler for fish is in the form of an iron standard, eighteen inches in height. It stands on three long slender legs and has a cross bar near the top of the standard. On this cross bar are hooks on which birds also could be hung. This could have been used for meat, too.

The wafer iron and the waffle iron date back to the fourteenth century and were used in the old country in church services. They had long handles with two heads, shutting like pincers. The waffle iron had oblong heads, of different sizes, while the wafer iron had round or elliptical heads. The waffle iron, just as today, had a waffle pattern on each head, which gave it its name; later ones made in factories have a number and date of manufacture. The wafer iron had a design on each head, consisting of scrolls or other patterns, initials, dates and hex marks. The hex mark was put on various implements, tools and utensils, and even over doorways, with the hope of keeping off the evil spirits. Both the waffle iron and the wafer iron were used early in this country, first in church services and later in the home. It was customary to give a bride a wafer iron on which were her initials, the date of the wedding and a hex mark for luck. These irons are further described in Chapter Four.

A flip dog always hung by the chimney. Other names for this long iron, used to heat the drink of flip or toddy in front of the huge fire, were hottle and loggerhead. The iron was first heated in the embers, and when thrust into the drink, red-hot, it made the drink sizzle and gave it a pleasing burnt taste. These irons were from two to three feet in length and there seem to have been two types: one with a tear-shaped end and the other with a pointed end. A looped handle made it possible to hang it along with the other fireplace equipment, and when hot drinks were man's best friend, the flip dog was the most popular implement that hung there ready for use.

Bellows or belluses, used to fan to life a sickly blaze, were, of course, necessary additions to the fireplace. They are said to have originated in Scythia in 600 B.C., conceived by Anacharais, a philosopher. The earliest bellows were a fire-blowing tube. In China and Japan the tube was a bamboo stalk, and in early England it was metal, standing on a base with two small feet, with a handle by which it was held as it was used. John Smith brought bellows made of goat skin to this country in 1624; and it was not long before they were elaborately made of wood and leather, with brass tacks, and ornamented in gay-colored designs. Fans and turkey wings were used to help the fire when a pair of bellows was not available.

The hearth was kept clean with brooms of various sorts. Turkey wings could be used; but the most common broom was made by tying brush twigs to a wooden handle, although the splintered birch broom was often found at the hearth. Any of these could be easily replaced.

The Dutch crown was an invention used in the larder that held smoked meats and prepared meats to be frozen. It was made with a band of brass or wrought iron, on which were six or seven hooks. From these arms extended to a central point where there was a ring by which the crown was suspended from the ceiling on a cord. One large hook with two prongs hung from the center. The crown could be lowered and raised as needed. Food was set away to freeze for the winter months, and it was necessary to have a suitable arrangement by which it could be stored. A few Dutch crowns are still in existence, but they are not commonly seen; one is in Gore Place in Watertown, Massachusetts, and one in Wells Museum at Sturbridge, Massachusetts.

FLIP DOGS, USED FOR HEATING THE DRINK OF FLIP OR TODDY, ALWAYS HUNG BY THE CHIMNEY. THE ONE WITH HEAD BENT, SO MADE FOR EASIER HEATING OF THE BEVERAGE, IS THE OLDER OF THE TWO.

THE COLONIAL HEARTH WAS KEPT CLEAN WITH A VARIETY OF BROOMS. TURKEY WINGS BOUND AT THE HANDLE WITH BLACK CALICO WERE FREQUENTLY USED.

There were, in the early days, an endless number of skimmers of brass and iron, with large heads and small heads, long handles and short handles. So, too, were there meat forks and hooks, to take the meat from the kettles and pots, or to test cooking meats and birds. Long and short three-pronged hooks were made, either to use in hanging meats when cooking, or to set in a cool well to hold buckets of milk or butter.

The many utensils and contrivances in use gave the blacksmith much to do, for it was he who not only fashioned but also created on his anvil after the colonists had become established in their new homes.

It would be impossible for one person to carry on research work on fireplace utensils and implements throughout the entire country. The descriptions given in this chapter cover such equipment in a general way, but there are doubtless dozens of different types scattered in museums and historical buildings. Also, each locality without doubt had its own names by which these were called, unknown to other localities. This was inevitable in the early times.

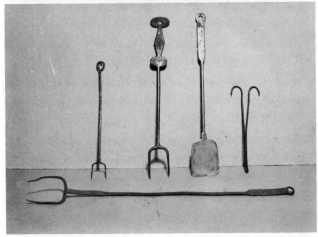

(*Top*) These spatulas of tin, wood, and iron once did yeomen service in turning griddle and oat cakes. (*Below*) The village blacksmith showed his inventive talents in this group of useful meat forks, and a spatula.

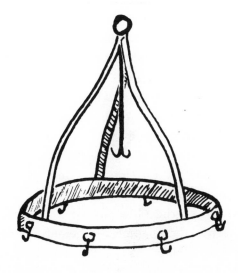

On this Dutch crown, ten or fifteen inches in diameter, meats were hung in the larder. It could be lowered and raised by means of a rope.

81

IV

Food and Drink in the Old Days

THE TASKS THAT confronted the early settlers when they cleared the land, built their homes, tilled the ground, planted, raised their families and faced each day's obligations gave little time for relaxation. One often thinks of those early years as full of peace, serenity and happiness, whereas there was little but hardships, privations and a struggle for sheer existence.

Little time was taken for eating in those first years. Much thought and long hours were spent on the preparation of food, but the act of eating at mealtime was most unceremonious and done in short order. Savages ate when hungry, using their fingers and an occasional spoon, and those early white men who came to the wilds of America, while far advanced from savagery, were primitive in their manner of eating.

Kettles and pots swung on the wooden lug pole in the fireplace, ready with the food for the morning meal, and each one of the family helped himself and ate until satisfied. There was not always plenty. The day was started off with a mug of beer or cider and a bowl of porridge — cornmeal pudding called mush, pap, Indian pudding and hasty pudding. This was eaten with milk, or possibly with maple-syrup molasses; and when butter became a possibility in the home, that too was added to the pudding.

It took hours to cook the pudding properly, and it was prepared the night before and left in the kettle, cooking slowly over the covered fire, to be ready for morning. The name hasty pud-

ding is most deceptive when applied to that mess of porridge, for it needed long, slow cooking over the embers. Children were given the task of stirring it in the big iron kettles. Long-handled wooden spatulas with small flat heads were used, and an occasional spoon has been found with a nose snubbed from being used standing on end in stirring. Spatulas or stirrers for the Indian pudding were called "porridge paddles"; many were the stirrers used in those big kettles, for everything from pudding to soap.

Some form of bread, too, was eaten at breakfast — the bannock cakes or hoe cakes, baked in front of the fire, or the rye and corn-meal bread called "rye and Injun," baked in the three-legged Dutch oven.

Breakfast had little ceremony, being what the name implies — breaking the fast of the night, and it took place in the small hours of the morning by candlelight, except in summer. A wooden bowl, a wooden spoon and a wooden noggin or a gourd were all the utensils needed for the meal. The noggin was common property, and was passed from mouth to mouth. Stools and benches were in the room, but to sit or to stand was a matter of choice, and with the day's work lying ahead, no time was lost over the bowl of pudding.

Customs of the old country were carried on in the new land, some of them remaining almost unchanged for many years. Because water was little used as a drink in their native lands,

THE CENTRAL PIECE OF FURNITURE IN THIS NEW YORK STATE CABIN IS A HUTCH TABLE OPENED UP AS A SETTLE. THIS WAS A POPULAR AND USEFUL TYPE OF TABLE IN THE EARLY COLONIAL HOUSE. A LET-DOWN BED IS SEEN AT THE RIGHT.

it was not considered by the colonists as fit to be used as a beverage. The English clung to their ale, the Dutch had their beer, and the Spanish and the French their light wines. But beer could be brewed so readily with barley and hops, or such roots as ginger, spruce and sassafras, that these were the drinks commonly used in homes of the colonists. Another reason why water was not considered a suitable drink was because of the unsanitary condition of the villages for many years.

With the coming of the fruit trees, brought over on ships shortly after 1630, apple orchards were planted and the yield of apples increased every year. It was then that beer disappeared from the tables and cider was used freely in every home. A man was rated by the number of barrels of cider he could leave in his will, and he often had several hundred. There was always a free barrel of cider in the cellar for Indians and white strangers alike, and it goes without saying that it was replenished frequently. Even children drank cider, and when it was left un-adulterated, or when it had not become too "hard," it was a harmless enough drink.

The type of table on which the food was

INDIANS WERE ADEPT AT FASHIONING WOODEN UTEN-
SILS SUCH AS THIS WELL-PRESERVED BURL BOWL FROM
THE COLLECTION OF A. B. WELLS.

running through each standard. This was called
a trestle table, or more often a "table bord," because the top was one board. Pulling out the
stretcher released the standards, and when they
were folded down the board could be stood
against the wall. The family sat at one side only.
In this connection, it is interesting to note that
the painting, "The Last Supper," shows Christ
and his disciples sitting at such a table, all on
one side.

THIS HUGE BURL BOWL MADE AND USED BY THE
INDIANS MAKES AN INTERESTING COMPARISON IN SIZE
WITH THE EATING BOWL AND HOUSE MORTAR USED
BY THE COLONISTS. *A. B. Wells.*

eaten was the result of the crowded condition
of the "hall," or kitchen, and it could be put out
of the way when not in use. If the man of the
house did not happen to be handy with his tools
to the extent of making furniture, a cabinet
maker was called on, and butter and cheese were
bartered in exchange. One style of table was a
thick, wide, oaken plank set on three standards
that were fastened together by a long stretcher

IN EARLY AMERICA A LARGE CENTRAL WOODEN BOWL
WAS THE RECEPTACLE FOR STEWS AND SIMILAR CON-
COCTIONS AND FROM IT EACH ONE HELPED HIMSELF.
THE BOWLS WERE MADE ON A LATHE BY THE MAN
OF THE HOUSE. THIS BOWL IS FROM THE COLLEC-
TION OF THE LATE CHARLES HOPKINS.

Another popular and more useful type of
table was what was known as a hutch table. (See
page 83.) The word hutch means a compart-
ment or an enclosure, and this type of table was
a combination of settle and table, with a base not
unlike a small chest on bracket legs. There were,
in those early homes, all too few compartments
or chests in which to stow things away. The back
of the settle swung on wooden pegs and could
be tipped down to rest on the arms to form the
table top. Sometimes the back was square, sometimes round. At mealtime the settle was pulled
into the middle of the room and the back
dropped down, and the piece of furniture became a table ready for the meal. When the meal
was over, back it went again to serve as a settle.
Today such hutch tables are highly prized.

Another type of table which came in later
years was the one with drop leaves or folding
leaves. This, too, allowed for more space in the
room when the table was not in use and the

leaves were dropped, and it was the forerunner of the beautiful gate-legged table, which has several legs in the form of gates that can be folded shut.

A custom of the old country, but one that was never followed in this country, was that of making a table top with places cut in it that served as bowls. The plank was about six inches thick and the holes were bored about eighteen inches apart, one for each person, doing away with need of bowls.

The bowls used by the colonists were of all sizes, and there was a bowl for each member of the family. A large central bowl held stews and such food, and from this each one helped himself with his own bowl. The bowls were made on the lathe and the man who made this wooden ware was called a dish-turner. The man of the house or even the young boys sometimes could turn out such ware.

Wooden plates were made on the lathe, those brought from across the water being square, while those made here were usually made round. The square ones had indentations in each corner to hold the salt and other condiments, and the English often decorated their wooden plates with inscriptions around the flat part of the outer edge. A custom brought to this country, but which might have nat-

THESE TWO BREAD BOARDS AND A BUTTER DISH ARE DECORATED WITH CARVED INSCRIPTIONS READING "THE STAFF OF LIFE", "BUTTER", "SPARE NOT".

urally sprung up here even without previous usage, was that of turning the plate over and eating the dessert on the other side. Thus it came about that the two sides were called the "dinner side" and the "pie side." Perhaps the custom was New England in its thrift.

The wooden plates were called trenchers, as mentioned in Chapter One, the name coming from the old French word meaning to cut or carve. New England thrift required that more than one person eat from a trencher, and man and wife or several children had to partake of their food sharing the same trencher. If by chance a young woman and a young man ate from one trencher, they were considered engaged. It is said that in one town a new inhabitant whose trade was the making of wooden ware allowed each member of his family to have an individual trencher, and the magistrates of the town were highly indignant at his extravagance and reproved him severely. The word "trenchermate" naturally followed when two persons ate together, and the term "trencherman" was used when a person ate very heartily, somewhat as we use the word gourmand today.

IN THIS GROUP ARE TWO FAMILY AND FOUR INDIVIDUAL SALTS THE LARGEST OF WHICH IS SIX INCHES IN DIAMETER. THE ONE IN THE FOREGROUND IS MADE OF BURL.

THIS UNUSUAL BOWL WAS DEFTLY CARVED OF BURL. FROM THE COLLECTION OF A. B. WELLS.

85

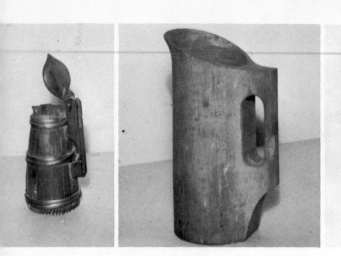

THE SMALL WOODEN JUG AT THE LEFT WAS USED FOR SYRUP FOR GRIDDLE CAKES AND WAFFLES. THE WOODEN NOGGIN (*center*) TURNED ON A LATHE, WAS USED AT ALL MEALS AND WAS PASSED FROM MOUTH TO MOUTH. THESE OLD GOURDS (*above*) FOUND IN ONE HOUSEHOLD, WERE USED AS DIPPERS. THE WHITE ONE DID DUTY AS A DARNING BALL.

The salt bowl of wood was of no small dimensions, being five or six inches in diameter. Salt came to the home in coarse form and had to be pounded in the mortar before it could be used. Salt boxes were kept by the chimney for use in cooking and the big salt bowl stood on the table. Individual salts appeared in due time, but the large salt bowl held sway for many years. It is recorded that Harvard University was given a "great silver salt" in 1644 (Harvard was founded in 1636).

It was the custom to use the salt as a dividing line when company sat at the table — those of high rank above the salt and those of low rank, and also children, below. At Harvard, the position of the salt differentiated the faculty and graduates from the understudents. Salt was mined in New England and in the South at an early date, and many men amassed a fortune by evaporating salt water and by mining for salt. A fine-grain salt was produced for the table and a coarse-grain salt for cattle.

Wooden porringers and those of pewter were used, the latter coming from the old country and being cherished along with the few plates of pewter. The wooden noggin was used at all meals and was passed from mouth to mouth. But noggins were also made in sets, consisting of two cups or three cups, made on a lathe and finished by hand; frequently there were eight sides, cut with a knife. The practice of drinking from one cup has not been laid aside for as many years as one might think. Some

church communions until quite recently used one cup for all, and this custom may still hold true in some small communities.

Leather bottles were used, as were leather cups, made from hides of various animals. The edge of the cup was sometimes bound with a band of tin — such a cup was called a black jack.

Sugar bowls of wood must have been graceful additions to the table. Some old bowls that we see today are as much as fifteen inches in diameter. Maple sugar was plentiful and was all that was known for many years. Even when white sugar was imported, and when sugar later was cultivated in the South, white sugar was used only on special occasions, such as the minister's call and holidays. White sugar came to the home in the form of a pyramid block and was cut into small pieces with special cutting scissors, which had two sharp heads that turned inward. If the sugar was used in cooking, it was first crushed in the mortar with a pestle.

The molasses-like syrup, drawn from the maple sugar that had been packed in tubs as soft sugar, was used on the table and in cooking. A small wooden jug made like a tankard testifies to the fact that syrup, used on griddle cakes and waffles, was popular in appeasing the appetite.

(*Above*) WOODEN SUGAR BOWLS USED ON THE TABLES WERE GRACEFUL IN DESIGN. SUGAR CAME IN BLOCKS AND WAS CUT BY SPECIAL SCISSORS. PORRINGERS (*upper right*) WERE IN CONSTANT USE. IN THE EARLY DAYS SHELLS AND HOLLOWED-OUT NUTS (*lower right*), TO WHICH HANDLES WERE ATTACHED, WERE USED FOR SPOONS AND DIPPERS.

In the author's collection is a sugar bowl, received as a gift, which came from across the water, its definite source not yet identified. The bowl has an elaborate standard, and a grooved neck and a cover. Around the sides of the bowl, four tiny mirrors have been set in ivory rings, with two ivory studs between each mirror. The cover has the same number of mirrors and studs, and the knob is of ivory in the shape of a fluted crown. The outside of the bowl is stained in a dark finish; the inside is light in color, like natural wood, though what kind of wood is hard to determine. In many instances, a foreign wood is found in the collection and is not easily catalogued; the wood of fruit trees was often used in wooden ware.

Pewter utensils, brought from the old country, were used in conjunction with wooden ware. Plates, porringers, salts, pitchers, platters, shallow bowls and drinking mugs of pewter stood on the kitchen cupboard when not in use. Many homes of wealth did not use wooden ware, but families in the early settlements, in the newly opened-up sections and those living outside of villages, away from the centers of transportation, continued for nearly two centuries to use wooden ware at the table. As late as the Revolution, wooden tableware was advertised for sale,

and during the war pewter all but disappeared, for it was taken as material for bullets.

China did not appear for general use until the eighteenth century, and then it was only in homes of the well-to-do that it saw regular service. In homes of lesser wealth, china was relegated to the closet in the parlor, to be taken out and used only on state occasions. The first china was brought over by the settlers and was highly prized by the owners. Then whaling vessels returned from foreign lands with such ware, thus constantly adding to the supply.

A story is told of a boys' school in England that had always used wooden plates. One morning the boys came to the table and saw their food on china plates. A general resentment was felt and without saying a word the boys with one accord slid their food onto the table — a wooden board — and, standing up, raised the china plates above their heads and at a signal from their leader dropped them onto the floor. Still not speaking, they sat down and ate their food from the table. The next meal brought forth the wooden plates again.* The hold of custom is very strong in the human race, in both young and old, and usually it is only by a slow process of evolution that changes can be satisfactorily brought about.

Eating implements did not find their way to the table for many years. A spoon was the only actual necessity, and for this the white settlers, like the Indians, used shells attached to a

* Correspondence of Frank K. Swain, Doylestown, Pa.

wooden handle. Often a nut was used instead of a shell; and long gourds, the fruit of the calabash tree, were hollowed and used as spoons, ladles and dippers. Perhaps the simplest spoon was made from a stick of wood, with a jackknife. Pewter spoons and those of alchemy, an alloy containing much brass, were made in wooden molds.

Porridge was eaten with a spoon, as were the meats, which were served as hash, highly seasoned ragouts, thick stews and hotchpotch, to all of which were added vegetables. The word hotchpotch readily turned into the modern "hodgepodge." Animals and birds roasted over the fire were eaten with the fingers. Pewter and alchemy spoons came to the table later.

Knives, of course, were used before forks, for they were necessary in cutting meat. Many a guest would produce his own knife, a jackknife, from his vest pocket and use it when in difficulty. One reads that Governor Winthrop of Boston owned a fork in a case in 1633; this was a rare thing at that date. By another half-century, forks with two tines had appeared, but were not used in the same manner as today. The fork merely held the meat, while the knife cut and conveyed it or other food to the mouth, the broad tip being used for that purpose. This custom is seen today among those of little education, and the explanation for it is that it is really an old custom which has never been entirely abandoned.

THREE OLD SUGAR BOWLS FOUND IN NEW ENGLAND HOUSES. THE ONE ON THE RIGHT IS SAID TO BE A RUSSIAN IMPORTATION. THE SUGAR BOWL ON THE LEFT WAS MADE OF WOOD AND TURNED ON A LATHE. BOWL IN CENTER, FROM PENNSYLVANIA, IS OF TIN AND HAS A PAINTED DESIGN.

OF THESE TWO UNUSUAL TANKARDS, THE ONE AT LEFT HAS A DECORATIVE INLAY OF HICKORY STRIPS. THE RIGHT ONE IS OF PENNSYLVANIA ORIGIN.

Children had no place at the table for many years. It is said that they stood behind their elders and received portions of food, or stood at their own places instead of sitting. They were not allowed to speak or to ask for food, and this custom of excluding children lasted for many years in some localities, especially among the wealthy. Children often had a small table of their own, which is sometimes customary today.

When Harvard University opened its doors to the first students in 1642, each pupil furnished his own pewter mug and wooden trencher.* Nothing is said about spoons, but it can be inferred that they were made by the boys from the woodpile; students had to supply their own wood, besides all of the food for the entire year. Breakfast was served at five o'clock in the morning and consisted of bread and beer. The meal was called bever, a word from the Old English, meaning a light lunch, or light meal, and light it was by any standards of today. Two meals a day were served at first, the second being supper in the late afternoon, and consisting of meat pie, hasty pudding with bacon, oatmeal porridge, a dish of eggs and beer. Records show that in 1657 the students drank 270 barrels of beer; but remembering that water was not used as a drink, this would not seem excessive to

* Samuel Eliot Morison, *The Tercentenary of Harvard College.*

COLOR ADDS TO THE GLORY OF THIS STAVED TANKARD FOR IT IS PAINTED RED. THE LITTLE WOODEN MUG, FOR TODDY AT THE FIRESIDE, HAS A SET-IN BOTTOM.

quench the thirst of the students, who not only studied but did the work of running the college farms.

Later a third meal, dinner, was added in the middle of the day, and that again consisted of meat, hasty pudding, dumplings, a vegetable, and beer. It was a cue of beer that each student was allowed, all that could be bought for a farthing or sometimes half a farthing. When such an allotment was given out, it was marked with a letter "Q" in the book called the "buttery book."

The lowly but all important cornmeal went into hasty pudding, also called Indian pudding or mush, as mentioned earlier, and this was served twice a day in every home, both rich and poor. Besides being served with milk, butter or syrup, it was later also fried on the flat iron griddle, like buckwheat cakes.

Porridge is mentioned in the Bible as pottage: "Then Jacob gave Esau bread and a pottage of lentils" (Genesis xxv, 34); and also Esau sold his birthright for a mess of potage. Many were the porridges in Colonial days. From cornmeal came suppawn, samp, hominy and succotash. Suppawn was a thick porridge of cornmeal and milk cooked together, and a favorite dish on the tables of the Dutch and the Southern colonists. Samp, or Indian nawsamp, like a coarse hominy, was made by crushing the ker-

nels in the mortar, boiling the mess and eating it hot or cold with milk or with butter. The Indians had a special mortar for samp, which differed from others in that it had a shallow cavity. The word succotash comes from the long name the Indian gave to corn, "suquttahhash," which now refers to corn and beans. Another food was sowens, which was sifted oatmeal allowed to sour in water and then boiled to a jelly.

The white man learned from the Indians how to till the soil, fertilize it with dead fish, plant the corn and harvest it. But the Indian was not a good provider and often went hungry, having eaten all of his corn. Then he would beg from the white man, or barter skins and beads for the precious kernels.

Parched corn beaten to a powder was carried in knapsacks on journeys, and it is said that three spoonfuls a day, taken with water or snow, was sufficient to sustain a man. It is not mentioned how large the spoons were. This was called nocake, from the Indian word nookick or nookhik. It is recorded that at a time of famine in the first years of the settlement, the Pilgrims were allotted only five kernels of corn apiece for food for one day.

Corn was taken as taxes and was considered legal currency, like gold and silver. It was used in trading with the Indians in exchange for skins, and also as ballots in the meetings — a kernel of corn was a "yea" and a bean was a

HERE IS A SAMPLE ASSORTMENT OF WOODEN TABLEWARE THAT WAS IN COMMON USE THROUGHOUT THE COLONIES. SPOON HOLDERS SUCH AS THE ONE PICTURED HERE FREQUENTLY WERE POLISHED TO A HANDSOME FINISH.

THE FIRST CORN SHELLER WAS A BARREL MADE FROM A HOLLOWED-OUT TREE TRUNK. THE BIG CORN SHELLER BARREL AT LEFT WAS MADE FROM THE SOUR GUM TREE WHICH WAS THE MOST PREFERRED. THE IMPLEMENT ABOVE IS A PESTLE OR POUNDER WITH WHICH THE EARS OF CORN WERE STRUCK.

"nay." Games were played with the kernels, and that of "hull gull, how many," which is now played with pebbles, originally had kernels for counting.

The best ears of corn were laid aside for seed, and the husks turned back and braided. This was called "tracing," and provided a means by which the corn could be hung in attics, sheds and barns. Shucks were used for stuffing in mattresses and for making a braided mat for the back entry.

The corn was shelled from the cob by rubbing the ears against the edge of a shovel or tub, or even the edge of a large frying pan. The first corn sheller was a barrel made from a hollowed-out tree trunk. This had a bottom of rods that acted as a grating, or a board floor in which holes had been bored with a gimlet. If possible, a sour-gum tree was used for the barrel, for this tree becomes hollow as it grows old. Thus the task of making a barrel was greatly simplified — one merely cut a tree trunk in the desired length and polished it inside and outside. These barrels were used for receptacles as well as for corn shellers.

The ears of corn were dumped in and pounded with a large pestle, the kernels falling through the rods or holes and the cobs remaining on the bottom. Some pounders we see today have a heavy head on a handle, while others have a shaped head (illustrated this page). The cobs were used in making a smudge to smoke hams.

Another sheller was made of two slabs of wood filled with headless nails. One slab was fastened to an easel, and the other slab, which had a protruding handle, was pegged to the fastened part, playing freely. The ears were held between the two slabs and as they were rubbed between them, the kernels ran down into a basket placed below.

The kernels were ground for meal, the first primitive method being a stone mortar and a stone pestle. Large circular stones were chosen and a hole was made in the center to hold the stones together on an axle. The stones were rough, the better to grind. First this was done by hand power, then by horse power, and later by wind power and water power. The meal was kept in bins in the barn, and in barrels or tubs in the buttery. Some corn was grown for popping corn or "pop corn."

In the early colonies, dinner was served at twelve noon; though on the farms it was an hour earlier. It might be mentioned here that time was reckoned by the shadows of the sun, and this brought about the making of sundials in the colonies. There is in the author's collection an old peg-calendar which told the days of the month, as well as one for the days of the week. The one for the days of the month is a smooth, thin stick of wood, a foot long and two inches wide. Thirty-one holes were cut, in two columns, one hole for each day of the month, each day being noted by a shoe peg, moved from hole to hole. The calendar stick for the days of the week is smaller. Indian pudding was the first course at dinner, followed by meat, vegetables and bread.

Bread varied greatly in the ways of mixing or baking. There were the hoe cakes of the South, the ash cakes of the North. Those of the South were baked in front of the fire on the head of a hoe; those of the North were first baked in ashes in the manner of the Indians, who had pits lined with stones and heated by fire.

Bannock cake, or the bannock bread of the North, was baked on a small board propped in front of the fire, resting against a kettle or on its own handle. The board was called a bannock board or merely a bakeboard, and not all of them have been relegated to the wood pile. Another name for such cakes was "jonny cakes," the spelling being shortened from the word journey, because the cakes were carried on journeys. Our johnny cake of today is the same thing, having acquired merely a change in spelling.

Bread made with yeast is mentioned in writings by the middle of the eighteenth century. To describe the liquid yeast is like trying to unravel a ball of yarn to find the beginning. The yeast was kept in a glass or an earthenware crock, and part of the first lot was passed from grandmother to mother to daughter. From *Candle Days*, by Marion Nicholl Rawson, come some rules to this effect: "Boil potatoes, wash and mix in a tablespoon of flour, then sift through a colander. Then put in a cup of yeast reserved from the old. Also pour hop water into this."

Another rule says: "Put water in a frying pan. Everybody raised hops in the old days and stripped them off. (Author's note: They were kept in large baskets as they dried.) You put one

This ingenious sheller, for rubbing the kernels of corn from the cob, is from the Rufus Putnam house at Rutland, Massachusetts.

in . . . then slice up thin two smallish potatoes, let them cook together until done . . . Then mash potatoes and sift into a dish, then put in some of the old yeast and the salt. To keep it, add cornmeal, roll out flat and then cut into little flat, hard strips — lay away in a jar."

One discovers that in the original batch of yeast, "emptyins" were used. This was the settlings of beer barrels. Also the froth that came when mash was made could be taken. Whatever was used had to be something that was fermented. Thus, "we come to the conclusion that yeast is made by a combination of potatoes, salt, hops and heat, mixed with an understanding and sympathy which cause fermentation to set in, and behold — the great leavener of the staff of life, yeast forever and forever, on the kitchen shelf."

In some sections of New York, Pennsylvania and the South, there were bake houses, where great amounts of food were baked. The big ovens took much work away from the kitchen. This was the same idea as the village bake shop in New England, in the cellar of a tavern.

Pumpkins, or "pompions," were the fruit of a trailing plant, and were found growing wild. The Indians dried the pumpkins, cut them and strung the pieces for winter use, and in this manner the colonists also kept them. They were used in bread, made half and half with Indian meal; but because of its coarseness such bread was none too popular. In fact, pumpkins were rather held in disfavor, and even in times of famine they were not eaten with relish. They were stewed and were made into sauce, and in the South they were mixed with other vegetables such as corn, peas and beans.

A favorite way of cooking them was to cut off the stem and a small part of the top, scoop out the seeds and the soft center part and bake the shell in the oven. Milk was poured in when it was served. An old cookbook says to "slice them when ripe and cut them into dice and so fill a pot with them of two or three Gallons and stew them upon a gentle fire the whole day. And as they sink they fill again with fresh Pompions, not putting any liquor to them and when it is stir'd enough it will look like bak'd Apples, this dish putting Butter to it and a little Vinegar with some Spice as Ginger which makes it tart like an Apple and so serve it up to be eaten with fish or flesh." *

A list of vegetables used in those days includes many of the present day — beans, peas, carrots, parsnips, turnips and potatoes. The story of potatoes is interesting, and rather strange. It was thought, when they were first known, that eating them would cause death after seven years, and that if cattle or horses ate them, they, too, would die. Only a few farmers ventured to plant them, and then only a few bushels; all that were left in the spring were burned. In the beginning, potatoes were cooked as a main dish, rather than as a vegetable, being mixed with butter, sugar, grapejuice, dates and lemons, and seasoned with spices such as mace, cinnamon, nutmeg and pepper, and then frosted

* Alice Morse Earle, *Early Colonial Days*.

over with sugar. This concoction left little taste of potatoes!

Potatoes journeyed across the ocean and back again before they were recognized as food in this country. They were carried to the old country and were grown in Ireland, becoming popular there. Then some Irish immigrants brought them to New Hampshire, and in that transportation they acquired the name of "Irish" potatoes. Aside from being a food, potatoes were used in making yeast and starch. Sweet potatoes were imported from Brazil and were grown extensively in the South, where the warm climate was suited to growing them. History says that the name "potato" was applied to this species before the commonly known white potato was used in the North. In the old days, sweet potatoes were roasted or were used in puddings, and often as a substitute for flour.

In making starch, the raw potatoes were grated and then put through a sieve. Both

THESE GRATERS WERE MADE FROM A "PAUL REVERE" LANTERN. THE BIG GRATER WAS FASHIONED FROM THE LARGER PART OF THE LANTERN, WHILE THE SMALLER ONE WAS MADE OUT OF THE LANTERN'S DOOR.

graters and sieves were made of tin, pierced with nails. The graters were made with a wooden handle and a wooden back, to the sides of which a curved piece of perforated tin was nailed. Sometimes the holes were made in a pattern. A Paul Revere lantern was converted into two graters, the body and the door each making a grater.

After the potatoes had been put through a sieve, they were cooked with water, and stirred with a wooden paddle so that the starch settled to the bottom of the kettle. The water was poured off and the layer of starch dried thoroughly and then washed again. The starch paste was then laid on porous bricks or slabs of gypsum, sometimes called alabaster, which was found in deposits in the soil. A finer starch, made from Indian corn was known as corn starch and was used in cooking.

No history of New England would be complete without telling of its bean porridge. The old childhood rhyme seems to have been traditional, having no title and no author.

> *Bean porridge hot,*
> *Bean porridge cold;*
> *Bean porridge in the pot,*
> *Nine days old.*

> *Some like it hot,*
> *Some like it cold;*
> *Some like it in the pot,*
> *Nine days old.*

The porridge was cooked in the deep bake ovens in large quantities, and some of it was set away to freeze. When taking a journey, the family would carry a good-sized portion of the frozen porridge to eat when hungry.

Eating bean porridge with brown bread made of corn meal became a custom on Saturday, and attached itself to Boston primarily, which gave the name of Bean Town to the old city in Massachusetts. There were village bake shops which helped out the busy housewife, and Saturday at noon the baker went his rounds and gathered the pots of beans, cooked them in the large oven located in the cellar of some tavern,

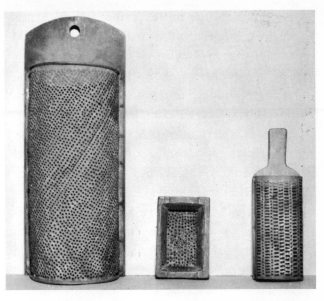

THE GIANT GRATER AT THE LEFT, TWENTY INCHES LONG, DWARFS THE ORDINARY TYPE AT RIGHT. THE FRAMED ONE IN THE CENTER WAS USED AS BOTH A GRATER AND A SIEVE.

and on Sunday morning returned the pot with brown bread to the rightful owners. Or the bean pots were often collected on Saturday morning and returned in time for supper that night. A man about seventy years old recalls today how in his childhood he had to carry the bean pot to a bake shop and go after it in time for supper. Historic Wright's Tavern, in Concord, Massachusetts, has a large bake oven in the cellar, at the base of the chimney, and in this room was the village bake shop, with one of the town's citizens serving as baker. (See page 65.)

From frugality and near-famine, living changed to an over abundance of food. After the first half-century of settlement there was plenty to be had, and the tables were heaped. One dinner reported mentions, among its desserts and relishes, flummery, jellies, sweetmeats of twenty sorts, trifles, whipped sillabubs, floating islands, fools, and then a dessert of fruit, raisins, almonds, pears, peaches and wines.

An old record shows that Judge Sewall, in the early 1770's, had a dinner of "Boil'd Pork, boil'd Pigeons, boil'd Venison, rost Beef, rost Lamb, rost Fowls, Joil of Salmon, Oysters, Fish and oil, conners, (known as cunners or blue perch) Legg of Pork, Hogs Cheek and souett;

pastry, bread and butter; minc'd Pye, Aple-pye; tarts, gingerbread, sugar'd Almond, glaz'd Almonds, honey, curds and cream, sage cheese, green peases, barley, Yokhegg (corn) in milk, Chockolett, giggs, oranges, shattucks, apples, quinces, strawberries, cherries and raspberries." Twenty-five were said to have sat at the table, and one marvels not only at the variety and the great amount of food, but also at the labor which such a meal entailed in preparation. Food and religion seem to have made up the most important part of life for many generations; and the preparing of food and the time spent in religious services must have taken up the biggest share of the daytime.

Again in the eighteenth century, in Philadelphia, the record of an elaborate meal listed: "three tureens turtle soup, several dishes stew with boned turkey, roast ducks, veal and beef." The table was then cleared and the dessert came, with two kinds of jellies, various kinds of puddings, pies, preserves, almonds, nuts, raisins, apples and oranges.

Supper was a simple meal, much like breakfast, the word itself meaning to sup, indicating a light meal. Again it was the Indian pudding and a drink, or plain bread and butter and a drink, which might be cider or beer. By 1630,

THIS WINE PRESS WAS DESIGNED LIKE A CHEESE PRESS. IT WAS USED FOR PRESSING OUT THE JUICE OF ELDERBERRIES AS WELL AS THE JUICE OF GRAPES.

when milk was plentiful and selling for only a penny a quart, it was added to breakfast and supper. Oatmeal and a pottle of milk was common by 1670 — a pottle meaning four pints, although originally meaning pot or tankard.

Tarts seem to have been a favorite sweetmeat, with fruits and berries growing over the land in wild profusion. Checkerberries, boxberries, gingerberries, huckleberries and grapes were to be had for the picking, a task assigned to the children and considered a regular duty for them. By 1630 apple trees had been planted and were soon bearing fruit, although the first of the planting was not successful. A short time later, apples were abundant and were used in many appetizing ways. They were made into pies and tarts, and sliced and dried for the winter; they were made into applesauce, with cider or apple-molasses or quinces added for variation. Many barrels of cider were stored for the winter by the thrifty settlers. Poor apples went into vinegar and a poor grade of cider; all of which made an apple orchard a profitable thing to possess.

Perhaps the first making of pies has never been recorded, but it is certain that in the colonies pies were a necessary part of the meal. It probably was a meat pie that was first made, and this developed into a mince pie, made especially for Thanksgiving. It was not always a thin, delicate crust that covered the pie, for often a coarse meal was all that was known when flour was stone-ground at home before the days of grist mills. To say what went into the meat pies would be a conjecture, for meat was taken from both wild and tame animals and birds — one writer tells of a Thanksgiving pie made of bear's meat and dried pumpkins, with a sweetening of maple sugar or sugar-molasses, and a crust of cornmeal and water.

Alice Morse Earle quotes a Swedish parson, Dr. Acrelius, who wrote home in 1758 in his account of the settling of Delaware: "Apple-pie is used through the whole year, and when fresh apples are no longer to be had, dried ones are used. It is the evening meal of children. House-pie, in country places, is made of apples neither

94

THIS CRUSHER, WITH A CORRUGATED ROLLER FOR GRAPES OR ELDERBERRIES, RESEMBLES A CURD BREAKER EXCEPT FOR A DIFFERENCE IN THE ROLLER.

peeled nor freed from their cores, and its crust is not broken if a wagon wheel goes over it."

Fruits and berries were used for pies as they are today, apples being the most popular, with wild blueberries, huckleberries, gooseberries and cherries close favorites. There were pies made from pumpkins and squash, and custard pies as well as those of mince meat.

The pies were made in large numbers at Thanksgiving time and set away to freeze for the months ahead, often as many as forty or fifty of them stacked one upon the other in the larder or pantry. When needed, they were thawed in the tin biscuit oven. New England's breakfast table never lacked a pie in the old days, and dinner and supper saw various pies served in huge portions, or, in the vernacular, huge slabs. The spelling at that time was "pye" or "aplepye."

From Pennsylvania comes a pie closet with pierced tin doors and sides, and with three shelves. This was a sanitary place for freezing the pies, the pierced tin allowing the air to circulate freely. One such pie closet is owned by Enid Louise Fairbairn of Wellesley, Massachusetts.

An interesting bit of history called "The Antiquity of Cookery" is found in Complete Housewife or Accomplished Gentlewoman's Companion, by E. Smith, London, 1747.

"Apples, nuts and Herbs were both meat and sauce. Man passed from a Vegetable to an Animal Diet (after 2 thousand years) and fed on Flesh, Fowls and Fish, then Seasonings grew necessary both to render it more palatable and savory, and also to preserve the part which was not immediately spent, from Stinking and Corruption; and probably Salt was the first seasoning discovered; for of Salt we read Genesis xiv.

"Cookery then began to become a Science, though Luxury had not brought it to the Height of Art. Thus we read that a Jacob made a palatable Pottage, that Esau purchased a Mess of it at the extravagant Price of his Birthright. And Isaac before (by his last Will and Testament) he bequeathed his Blessing to his Son Esau, required him to make some Savory Meat such as his Soul loved; i.e. such as was relishable to his blunted Palate.

"So that seasoning of some sort was then in use; though whether they were Salt, savoury Herbs, or Roots only, or Spices, the Fruits of Trees, such as Pepper, Cloves, Nutmegs; Bark of Cinamon, Roots, as Ginger, etc, I shall not determine.

"As for the Methods of the Cookery of those Times. Boiling or Stewing seems to have been the principle method; Broiling or Roasting next; beside which I presume scarce any other were used two thousands years and more; for I remember no other in the History of Genesis.

"That Esau was the first cook, I shall not presume to assert; but Esau is the first Person mentioned that made any Advances beyond Dressing, as Boiling, Roasting, etc. For tho we find, indeed that Rebecca, his Mother, was accomplished with the Skill of making savoury Meat as well as he, yet whether he learned it from her, or she from him, it is a Question too knotty for me to determine.

"But Cookery did not long remain a simple science or a bare Piece of Housewifery, or Family Oeconomy; but in Process of Time, when Luxury entered the World, it grew to an Art, nay a Trade: For in I Samuel viii, 13, when the Israelites grew Fashionists, and would have a King, that they might be like the rest of their

Neighbors, we read of Cooks, Confectioners, etc.

"The Art of Cookery etc. is indeed diversified, according to the Diversity of Nations or Countries."

There was much pickling and candying, with wild fruit so abundant and maple sugar plentiful. Spices came from far-off lands, but they were used by the colonists by 1640, when whaling vessels, taking out masts, salt and bricks, returned with many things not found in the new land. Spices were used in large quantities in preserving, the fruits being set in heavy syrup. Herbs, too, were brought back by trading vessels and were used freely in cooking and preserving, as well as in medicines. The growing of herbs in the gardens of the new country was soon begun, and the herbs were sold commercially, as well as used in the homes.

The Dutch made much of food and eating, and when they built homes there were large storerooms and larders provided — in fact, almost more space given to the provisions than to the family.

In addition to weddings, christenings and funerals, the Dutch had many festivals and seasonal affairs, and for each of these there were special kinds of sweetmeats. A cooky made especially for Christmas festivities, and called marzipan, or marchpane, was made of pounded almonds and sugar. It was stamped with a cooky print, cut with a pastry jigger and frosted with a decoration. Some of those wooden cooky prints or stamps are not unlike butter prints, being round in shape, and having a design cut in them, sometimes both sides having a design. Other prints were made in a set, an oblong block of square sections, with a different design in each square, though sometimes one pattern took the entire space. The latter were used principally for gingerbread, while the individual prints were for cookies.

The pastry jigger or pastry knife was a very old tool, used in Europe in the early seventeenth century. One has a wheel at one end and a curved cutter at the other, made of cast brass which cut the cooky dough. Some jiggers have a double wheel and no curved knife, the wheels being serrated and acting as cutters. The wooden pie crimpers of the colonists were made on a similar plan, with a wheel at one end; these were used to crimp the edge of pies. Some of the wooden pie crimpers had prongs at the end opposite the wheel, with which holes were pricked in the upper crust of the pies.

Waffles and wafers (see page 79) were made very early, as the old irons testify; and the waffle iron is listed as early as 1358 in England. Their original use was in connection with special church services. The irons, consisting of two long handles and two heads, were cast, and were extremely heavy. As mentioned earlier, the waffle iron had oblong heads and the wafer iron round heads, although later the waffle was square or heart-shape, the wafer was often oval.

History relates that in rural England in 1358 there was a Sunday in mid-Lent on which young people and children were admonished to visit their parents and to take wafers to their mothers. This was called Wafering Sunday or Mothering Sunday. In Sweden it was the waffle that was made for this occasion, which gave the name Waffle Sunday. A man who was given the

THE EARLY SPICE GRINDER AT THE LEFT HAS A PIECE OF TIN NAILED IN BOTTOM OF THE CUP AND ON END OF THE PESTLE; STEEL POINTS TAKE THE PLACE OF TIN IN THE ONE AT RIGHT.

task of making the wafers was called a "waferer." He had two or sometimes three wafer irons for the purpose. The irons were placed over the embers as the wafers baked, the long handles resting on a pot or kettle, and the length of them allowing the worker to keep back from the heat. All such iron utensils had handles two or three feet in length. A wafer iron of later date was used in a stove hole over the coals, as a short handle testifies.

A fourteenth-century rule for making wafers is very elaborate. It says to use the stomach of a full-grown pike, ground in a mortar with cheese, flour and whites of eggs beaten together, sugar and ginger; "put all together and look that the eyroun [iron] be hot and lay them in a thin paste and then make thin wafers and so on and on." Sometimes the wafers were not served flat but were rolled, as this rule of the nineteenth century would testify: "Dry flour well which you intend to use, mix a little pounded sugar and finely pounded mace with it; then mix it into a thick batter with cream; butter the wafer irons, let them be hot; put a teaspoonful of butter into them, so bake them carefully, and roll them off with a stick." * Later rules

* J. Seymour Lindsay, *Iron and Brass Implements of English and American Homes.*

were not so elaborate, and the batter is like that of the present day.

An old seventeenth-century rule for waffles reads: "1 pound flour, quarter pound butter, 2 eggs, beat, one glass wine and a nutmeg." The waffles had more substance to them than wafers, as the pattern allowed more batter for each waffle.

The custom of using the wafer iron for domestic purposes continued until the nineteenth century. In this country the observance of a special Sunday was not followed, but there were services in the church where the waffles were served. The custom of giving a wafer iron to a bride was common among the Dutch, and the date of the wedding and the initials of the bride were cut in the iron. The Dutch called the iron an "izer," and the cookies made with it were izer cookies. This brought the wafer iron as well as the waffle iron into the home, to be used in making cakes for the table.

A wafer iron in the author's collection is marked W. C. M., and has the date 1785, with a heart and fancy scroll work and two hex marks added to the cutting. The latter were to keep the evil spirits away. The cutting is not reversed, so on the wafer the initials and date were

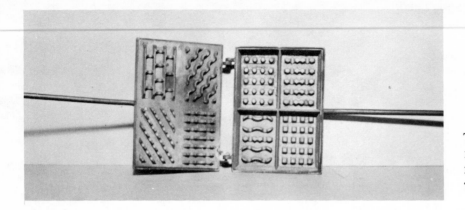

THIS WAFFLE IRON WITH LONG HANDLES IS UNUSUAL IN ITS INTRIGUING VARIETY OF PATTERNS.

marked opposite to the way they should lie. For scroll work it did not matter; but evidently the art of reversing letters and dates had not been conceived.

A griddle was an iron plate or pan used in cooking cakes. One of a later period is of soapstone, with an iron frame and handle. The cakes baked on these iron griddles were at first called just cakes. Then a thinner batter was made with a light flour or buckwheat flour and the cakes made from such a mixture were called griddle cakes, or buckwheat cakes.

When the white man first came to America, wild turkeys, geese and pigeons flew in large flocks. Turkeys weighed as much as forty or fifty pounds, and were seen from Maine to Virginia, affording a cheap and popular meal. Other birds included quail, pheasants, partridges, woodcock, snipe, plover and curlew, some being found in the woods and some by the water's edge. Similar birds were common to Old England, so the colonists were familiar with them and knew how to prepare them for the table.

Tin ovens appeared by the eighteenth century, with several types for the various things to be cooked or roasted. Turkeys and other large birds were roasted in the roasting oven, called a tin kitchen; small birds were hung by their breasts on hooks in a bird roaster.

Deer roamed the forest in large numbers; they were killed for food, and were often shared with the colonists by the Indians. It was the Indian who taught the white man how to shoot with bow and arrow and how to trap animals. The Indians never gave deer outright, but used them in exchange for things they wanted, especially rum, which they called the white man's "kill-devil." At the first Thanksgiving feast in December, 1621, the Indians brought five deer, joining the white man in giving thanks for an abundant harvest after the first severe winter of privations and sickness.

Squirrels and hares, or rabbits, were pests because they destroyed grain and they were killed and eaten with relish. An iron rabbit roaster (see page 74) was used in front of the fire, holding the dressed rabbit as it roasted. The hare, a larger species of the rabbit, abounded in the North, and also further west on the prairies.

Fish was plentiful in the ocean; and because the first settlements were located by the sea

GRIDDLES OF SOAPSTONE, LIKE THIS ONE WHICH WAS USED ON A STOVE, WERE NEVER GREASED.

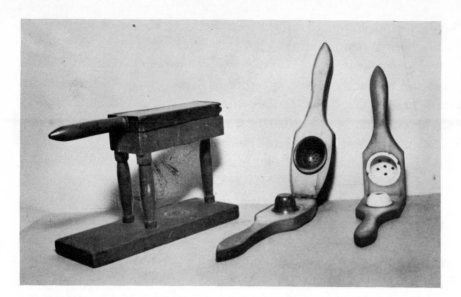

THE UNUSUAL LEMON SQUEEZER AT LEFT WAS MOUNTED ON LEGS TO ACCOMMODATE A TUMBLER BELOW. THE OTHER SQUEEZERS HAVE LIGNUM VITAE AND CHINA KNOBS AND CUPS.

coast, sea food appeared on the tables regularly. It has been said that there were more than two hundred varieties in New England waters alone. The Indians showed the white men their way of fishing, and also taught them how to prepare fish, as they had shown them how to cultivate and use corn. Fish were cooked on gridirons over the hot embers. Dead fish were used to enrich each hill of corn and to fertilize the soil in gardens.

Lobsters weighed twenty-five pounds apiece, and some caught in New York Bay were five or six feet long, according to records. One lobster supplied the family for a meal. Crabs and oysters were plentiful and large, and afforded food when other things were not to be had. Crabs measured a foot in length, and four men could be satisfied with one crab. Oysters, it has been authoritatively stated, were also large, being as much as a foot in length, and were pickled as well as roasted on gridirons for a meal. Both crabs and oysters were sent on trad-

ing vessels to the West Indies along with other supplies, for aside from their value as food, the shells supplied lime for making plaster.

Of the various fish caught in the waters of the sea, it was the cod which became the chief food for New England. The naming of Cape Cod came about because of the vast number of cod, for they literally filled the waters along the coast. The industry of cod fishing grew so rapidly that by 1640 three hundred thousand dried codfish were prepared for market in one year.

The expression, "on his own hook," comes from the trade of the fisherman, who was allowed only the fish which he caught on his own hook, as his share in the division of the lot. A young boy went out with the boat at the time of the big runs, and his share were the fish which had cut tails, this being something the boy himself did on each fish he caught. Because the boy cut out a piece of the tail, he was called a "cuttail"; but in time the boy grew into a skilled fisherman and might own a vessel of his own.

THESE FOUR PENNSYLVANIA COOKY PRINTS SHOW VARYING DESIGNS. THE LEFT ONE HAS A PATTERN ON EITHER SIDE; THAT IN THE CENTER A RAISED HANDLE, WITH PRINT OF A PINEAPPLE. THE PRINTS WERE PRESSED ONTO THE DOUGH AND A PIE CRIMPER OR PASTRY JIGGER, BOTH WITH A WHEEL, TRIMMED THE EDGE.

Saturday was fish day in New England, and no dinner was complete without codfish. When cod was cured in a particular manner to make it of a superior quality, it was called dun fish, and by that name the cod has frequently been called. Other popular fish were sweet mackerel, salmon, shad, bass, herring, haddock and eels, although none ranked in favor as did the cod, or dun fish.

Cod, shad and mackerel were "salted down" for the long months of winter; there was scarcely anything but what could be preserved in one way or another and set away in barrels, crocks or tubs, or hung in the open larder.

Domestic animals are mentioned very early, having been brought over on the ships following the *Mayflower*. The ship *Talbot* carried twelve mares, thirty cows and some goats, landing at Salem on July 29, 1629; while previous to that a bull and three heifers were referred to in 1624. Hogs and sheep must have followed in due season, for one reads of bacon, pork and sausages, and of lamb, veal and mutton; but there was little fresh meat eaten.

Meat was salted down in powdering tubs, and there was not a house but had a smoke oven where meat was smoked and put away for winter use. Smoked hams were kept packed in oats or surrounded by charcoal — the early settlers conceived many methods of preserving, having no other means of keeping food. Most of the large quantity of spices mentioned earlier was used for this purpose.

Cows provided much besides beef. The hairs of the tails were used in hair sieves; hoofs were powdered for the gluey substance which acted as a binder in making paint, and was called neats' foot, from the old name, neat, meaning cow. By 1634 milk was an important food, selling for a penny a quart. Hides of cows and calves were used as coverings for boxes and trunks, and were shredded for thongs which served as stout cords. A whole skin was used for an ox sling, a means of raising the oxen when they were to be shod. Even the horns of cows provided holders for powder, which were called powder horns, and were worn slung over the right shoulder and under the left arm. A horn to call the men to dinner was also made from an animal's horn.

Cows gave much variety in the way of food: liver, sweetbreads, heart, tongue, kidneys, meat for roasting, for steak and for the spit, as well as dried beef and corned beef. Whatever was left went into stews and ragouts.

Proof that bones were used comes from the old cookbooks. The Cook's Oracle, written in 1822 gives a rule for using the bones for the marrow. "Saw the Bones even, so that they will stand steady; put a piece of paste into the ends; set them upright in a saucepan, and boil til they are done enough; — a Beef marrow bone will require from an hour and a half to two hours, according to the thickness of the Bone. Serve fresh toasted Bread with them."

Another rule of a different sort is found in the Complete Housewife or Accomplish'd Gentelwoman's Companion. "To make marrow Pastries."

"Make your little Pastries the length of a finger, and as broad as two fingers, put in a large piece of marrow dipt in egg, and season'd with sugar, cloves, mace, and nutmeg; strew a few currants on marrow; bake or fry them."

At the time of the popularity of marrow bones, marrow scoops were found on the table.

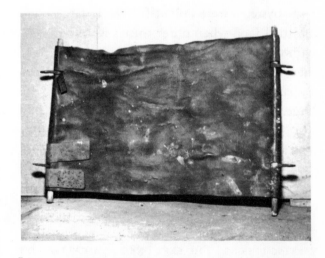

LARGE HIDES FOUR FEET LONG, FASTENED TO TWO POLES, WERE USED TO HOIST OXEN WHEN THEY WERE SHOD BY THE BLACKSMITH. THE HOOKS AT THE ENDS WERE SET INTO ROPES AND THE OXEN WERE RAISED BY THE USE OP PULLEYS.

These were long and slender, with a long gulley, to dig inside the bone and remove the marrow. These scoops were introduced at the time of Queen Anne and silver ones were made in great profusion. Iron ones were made for the kitchen, used when making marrow pasties.

Hogs, besides giving meat, supplied material for lard from the fat which lay next to the kidneys, and was shaped like a leaf. This lard, of the best quality, was called "leaf lard." The fat was tied in a bag, cooked in a kettle and then squeezed between a pair of wooden squeezers made for that purpose, and called lard squeezers. The grease ran into a wooden bowl and hardened as lard; many old wooden bowls show by the stain of grease that they were thus used. What was left in the bag was eaten as pork scraps, considered a dainty morsel, especially by the Dutch.

Hogs were killed once or twice a year and the hams were cured, smoked and stored away. Much of the meat was used in sausages, first chopped with a chopping knife. These, found in every pantry, were handmade and no two were alike, though they were only a piece of steel and a piece of wood. A collection of seventy of them in the author's museum shows the ingenuity of the men folk. One has a bone for a handle; one was made from the head of an ax; one was a foot scraper; one has two blades; one has two crossed blades.

Today, a sausage is minced meat in a cas-ing; in the early days a sausage was minced meat rolled into a finger-like cake and fried in deep suet. When minced meat was put into a casing, it was called hog's pudding. The old meaning of pudding was an intestine stuffed with meat, and a pudding was thus the main part of a meal, and not a dessert. Early cookbooks tell of these finger-like cakes fried in deep fat.

From the Complete Housewife comes a rule for "Very Fine Sausages":

"Take a Leg of Pork and Veal; pick it clean from skin and fat, and to every pound of lean meat put two pounds of beef-suet, pick'd from the skin; shred the meat and suet severally [separately] very fine; then mix well together and add a large handful of green sage very small, season it with grated nutmeg, salt and pepper; mix it well and press down hard in an earthen pot and keep it for use. When you use them, roll them up with as much egg as will make them roll smooth, but use no flour; In rolling them up, make them the length of your fingers; Fry them in clarified suet, which must be boiling hot before you put them in. Keep them rolling about in the pan; when they are fried through, they are enough."

Then came the time when minced meat was put into casings. Sometimes the small intestine was used for a casing; more often, the outside layer of the intestine was used because it was most transparent. This was cut in lengths of two yards each. After turned inside out with a candle rod, a slender wooden rod eighteen inches long, they were washed very thoroughly and scraped with a scraper. Then they were put into salt and water and soaked until used.

FOR GREATER CONVENIENCE IN OPERATING, THE PLATFORM OF THIS SAUSAGE GUN WAS MOUNTED ON LEGS.

Old cookbooks give many rules for hog's puddings, which were sometimes called blood pudding because the mixture was mixed with the blood of the animal. One rule read:

"Shred four pounds of beef-suet very fine, mix it with two pounds of fine sugar powder'd, two grated nutmegs, some mace beat, and a little salt, then pounds of currants wash'd and pick'd: beat twenty-four yolks and twelve whites of eggs, with a little sack; mix all well together, and fill your guts, being clean and steep'd in orange-flower water: cut your guts quarter and half long: fill them half full: tie each end, and again thus—oooo: boil them as others and cut them in balls when sent to the table."

The distinction between sausages and hog's puddings continued until the first quarter of the nineteenth century. In all the preparation of food there was an overabundance of spices.

When chopped meat was put into casings, the sausage gun appeared. It was a contrivance of tin, a long cylindrical tube with a snout, over which the intestine or gut fitted. A wooden plunger was used to push in the chopped meat; it was shaped somewhat like a potato masher, but with a long end. The sausage guns were home made, and various holders were rigged up to put the gun in when making sausages. One is a boxlike holder for a gun operated by a wheel with a handle. This rested on the table. There is also a gun four feet in length, with a hickory plunger that has a strip of leather wrapped around the end, to force out the meat. This long gun came from a tavern, and it held so much that one operation would make enough sausages for a meal. The illustration shows the comparison between the long gun and one of ordinary size.

Some ingenious man put his gun into a narrow platform on four legs. The gun sets into a hole; the plunger is cut short and the handle of the plunger sets into a long arm, playing on wooden pegs. The long arm is pegged into an upright at the end of the platform, which acts as a fulcrum. The stand made the labor of filling the cases less arduous, and the arm alleviated the work of forcing the meat into the gun.

Another device was a platform with no legs. This was placed on stools, but was not as convenient a contrivance as the one on legs, even though it could be stored away with less effort. Not all families owned a sausage gun, so the contrivance made the rounds when hog-killing time came and sausages were made for the winter.

The old cookbooks tell how hog's puddings were pricked when boiling. The filled intestines were tied at various distances, according to the length preferred. They could be cut in slices an inch thick and fried, or they could be tied so that they made balls when cut apart. To absorb the grease, puddings were placed on clean straw

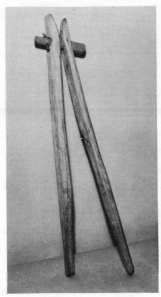

WITH HOGS AND GEESE ABUNDANT, LARD SQUEEZERS SUCH AS SHOWN ABOVE WERE IMPORTANT ADJUNCTS IN HOME ECONOMY. THE SAUSAGE GUN SHOWN AT THE UPPER RIGHT WAS BUILT INTO A CONTRIVANCE THE HANDLE OF WHICH OPERATED THE PLUNGER.

when taken from the kettle. Besides being a main dish, they were used to garnish fowls, hash or "fricasy."

Many rules for making hog's puddings are found in the old cookbooks. Each apparently strove to have the mixture that went into the casings be of surpassing excellence. The richer the better, it would seem, and the more the ingredients lent themselves to flavoring, the less one tasted the meat. In those days, there was a craving for spices and strong flavors in food and drinks.

Hogs were used as scavengers and roamed the streets. They were cared for by men called hog-reeves, whose duty it was to see that each hog was properly branded and had a ring in its nose, and that they did no damage to the crops. In those days crops were fenced in, just the opposite of the later custom of fencing in the cattle and livestock. When hogs roamed at will, gathering their food in the daytime, doors to houses were made in two sections, an upper and a lower, so that the lower part might remain closed while the upper part was opened. This was characteristic of house doors in Pennsylvania, and in New York where the Dutch settled; and such doors were often called Dutch doors.

Turkeys, ducks and geese became domes-ticated, and continued to be used as food. Wings from the turkeys were used as brushes for the hearth and feathers from the geese went into beds, bolsters and pillows, while the quills were used as pens.

A trick which the Indian taught the white man was that of stripping meat from animals, principally the bear, and drying it for food. With a sharp knife, the carcass was cut into, and then, catching an end of the flesh with his teeth, the Indian tore off a long strip. Such strips were hung on branches of a tree to dry in the sun, and when "cured" were stored as food for the winter. The white man did not resort to his teeth when stripping a carcass, but used a small sharp knife for the purpose. Such meat was called "jerk meat." In South America an industry of making this "jerk meat" was set up, and flourished for a considerable length of time.

By 1643, New England alone had 12,000 neat cattle, 3,000 sheep, 1,000 acres of orchards, and 15,000 acres under tillage. The first settlers were fishermen and farmers, for the villages were located by the sea and the land beyond was cleared for farms. Because of the denseness of the forests, villages pushed back from the coast very slowly. Another reason why new lands lay unexplored for so many years was the lack of means of transportation overland. Only the footpaths of the Indians connected one section with another, and they were little more than trails. On a highway on Marthas Vineyard, grotesque trees line the side of the road. The story is that in the days of the Gay Head Indians, the trails were marked by bending a young sapling a few feet from the ground, making a sharp right angle. As the trees grew, branches took an upright position from the horizontal part of the trunk and the bent trunks and the new growths make fantastic shapes. It is on Marthas Vineyard that, deep in the woods, one can still see the little burying ground of the Indians, beside a tiny white chapel. Two stones mark each grave: for adults there was a tall one for the head and a small one for the feet; for children, both stones were small. Each grave faces the west, for it was the Indian belief that they went west when they left the earth.

It was a fearsome thing to venture into the "forest primeval," with its tangle of undergrowth and its huge, tall trees; and many a stout heart hesitated before making new homes beyond the village boundary. In the South and in sections of New York there were small waterways and broad pasture lands, and villages sprang up more quickly than in New England.

Fully as important as meat was the milk that came from cows. Milk was plentiful by the beginning of the eighteenth century, and seems to have been commonly used on the table. At this time, one first finds churns mentioned in inventories. But butter is first mentioned in history as being used by the Arabs. When camels carried skins filled with milk on their backs, the motion of their rolling gait caused the globules of cream to coagulate and become butter. Like many great discoveries that have meant progress for mankind, this one was accidental.

There was scarcely any industry in the early colonies that required as much skill and time as did making butter and cheese. Each day, milk was poured into keelers — shallow tubs — to cool, and each morning cream was skimmed from the milk and put into the churns. This task fell to the children. When the churn was partly filled, the process of making butter was undertaken. This process is fully described in Chapter Five.

In the seventeenth century, few families owned churns, for butter was not a common food. It was not until the next century that both butter and cheese were made and eaten with any regularity, and as the years went on and the number of cattle increased, both commodities became staple foods.

Today a collection of churns shows much variety. The more common ones are those like deep buckets, narrow at the top, with a plunger that worked up and down, causing globules to form in the cream. A small churn, illustrated, was square in shape, and in one corner at the

THIS STANDING, RED-PAINTED CHURN WITH UPRIGHT HANDLE IS EQUIPPED WITH A SPLASH-CUP TO PREVENT CREAM FROM SPATTERING OUT.

HERE IS A GOOD EXAMPLE OF AN EARLY KEELER IN WHICH MILK WAS COOLED. *Skinner's Museum.*

and even ministers were paid with butter and cheese. When the village store came into existence, it was a customary thing for wagons to take their loads of produce, including butter and cheese, and exchange them for other necessary things for the home, such as spices, tea, coffee, calico and odd gadgets that appeared from year to year, and that pleased the fancy of the men folk as gifts for the children and the women. The custom of bartering has, in fact, never left the human race, although it sometimes goes by other names, that of swapping being the most common one of the present century.

Drinks other than water are almost as old as man. And all the kinds of drinks used since the days of primitive man could hardly be set down in print, because of their number. Fermented drinks and those unfermented have quenched the thirst of each generation and have stood for hospitality in all climes and in all places. When the white man came to the shores of the new land, he was so accustomed to his wine and ale and beer that he continued to have them here. Breweries were built in the colony that the Dutch settled, and stills were common to every section. When apples began to be plentiful, the colonists in the North gave up some of their drinks and used cider instead.

Water was not considered a drink, doubtless because of the unsanitary condition of the villages, so it was to the drinks that the settlers turned. And what could be more pleasing than a warm drink when the days were cold and the snow and wind chilled to the bone; or a cool drink in the heat of the day, when work in the fields was under way.

base is a small peg which pulled out to let out the buttermilk. Another illustration shows a rocking churn. This held a large quantity, and could be rocked either by the handles or by the rockers. If the housewife had sewing or needlework to do, or was holding the baby, she could keep the churn in motion with one foot. Another later churn turned by a crank, and it was not long before churns were turned by horse power.

Bartering with butter and cheese was a common way of obtaining what was not to be had from the land. Bartering began in the new country when the Indians came to the villages and traded skins and furs for beads, rum and vegetables, including corn, which the white man planted with more wisdom than did the carefree Indian, who gave little heed of the approaching winter.

Shepherds, lumbermen, coopers, peddlers

OF THESE TWO BUTTER CHURNS THE SQUARE ONE IS THE MOST UNUSUAL. IT HAS A PLUG NEAR THE BOTTOM TO LET OUT THE WHEY.

THE ROCKING CHURN WAS ROCKED BY ITS HANDLES OR BY THE PRESSURE OF A FOOT ON ITS ROCKERS. THIS ONE HAS A COVER IN CENTER WITH BUTTON FASTENERS.

Fruit drinks were made from pears and peaches, as well as from persimmons. Berries, barks, leaves and roots offered foundations for drinks; included among such sources were elderberries, juniper berries, sassafras bark, birch bark, spruce, hickory nuts, pumpkins and apple parings. The ingredients were mixed with water and with malt made from barley, and many were the combinations.

The names of some of the drinks were strange, and sprang into existence on the hearth; bellows-top, stone-wall, calibogus, black-strap and whistle-belly were some of the interesting names, impossible to be adequately defined. Switchel was molasses and water, unseasoned; metheglin or mead was a fermented beverage of honey, water, malt and yeast. In Virginia, the honey locust furnished a drink that was used in making metheglin.

Beer was imported at first, and later was made from imported malt and Indian corn. A native malt was obtained from hops and barley. Hops were grown in large quantities, were dried and stored in huge baskets and were sold for brewing purposes. One old home has a large basket in the loft of the lean-to, and there it must remain, for it cannot go through a window or a door. A molasses beer was made by using coarse sugar and molasses.

Flip was made by the fireside from beer and spirits or cider, heated with the iron flip-dog. The long-handled iron was first made red-hot in the embers, and then was thrust into the drink. It both heated the drink and brought it to a foam. Many a guest carried in his pocket a small, tin nutmeg grater so that he might flavor his own drink as he sat by a neighbor's fire.

Toddy, too, was drunk hot, differing from grog in that it was sweetened; it was stirred with wooden toddy sticks. There are many styles of toddy sticks, but all had a nub end on a short handle; they were used to crush the lemon, and to stir the spices and sugar in toddy. There were wooden, staved and hooped tankards, earthenware tankards, mugs of wood and earthenware, and glass and china mugs, all for the purpose of serving hot flip and toddy. Various punches were concocted when lemons could be had commonly, and these were served hot or cold.

Alice Morse Earle writes: "From persimmons, elderberries, juniper berries, pumpkins, corn-stalks, hickory nuts, sassafras bark, birch bark and many other leaves, roots and barks, various light drinks were made."

The wassail bowl was an ancient receptacle appearing on the table at a feast. It was large, and was made of silver or copper. The wassail, says Webster, was a "beverage formerly much used in England at Christmas and other festivities, made of ale or wine, flavored with spices, sugar, toast, roasted apples and so forth." It was mixed in the wassail bowl.

Caudle is defined as a warm drink for sick persons, made of wine, eggs, sugar and spices. But records show that it was also used at christenings, and one rule for making caudle reads: "Two gallons madeira wine, three gallons water, seven pounds sugar, oatmeal by the pound, spice, raisins, and lemons by the quart. Serve piping hot in large silver bowls with a silver spoon." For this, too, the wassail bowl was used.

Whiskey was made from rye, wheat or barley, and also from potatoes or corn. Wine was imported in large quantities, but after 1629 vineyards in the new country supplied domestic wine. Wild grapes, too, were plentiful. Every family had a wine press, which was a small press

TODDY STICKS, A VARIETY OF WHICH ARE SHOWN HERE, WERE USED TO CRUSH THE LEMON AND TO STIR THE SPICES AND SUGAR IN THE HOT TODDY.

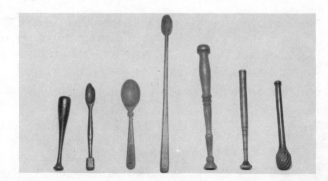

EVERY DRINK HAD ITS PROPER RECEPTACLE. HERE ARE A FLIP GLASS AND TODDY STOCK, A TIN TODDY CUP AND TWO STURDY TANKARDS.

made of wood, or of wood and tin. The juice of the grapes, extracted by the press, was fermented and made into wine.

Drinks of various kinds were served at funerals, weddings, huskings, ordinations and all social gatherings, including bees, for drinks were a part of the hospitality. Taverns and inns offered drinks to every traveler, and drunkenness was a common thing.

The story of rum has been called a vicious circle, and it was justly dubbed "kill-devil" and "fire-water" by the Indians. Sea captains and merchants took rum to the coast of Africa and bought slaves with it. Then the slaves were taken to the West Indies and sold to planters for molasses, which was brought back to New England and distilled into rum, which was used to start the journey over again. Eventually slaves were used in the Southern colonies; and New England, though she had no large estates calling for slave help, was only too willing to lend a hand in furthering the slave trade. Buying land with food and drink was a very common procedure. The town of Boxford, containing thousands of acres, was bought for nine pounds in money and "rum and vettels enuf." In 1757, Staten Island was sold by the Indians to the Dutch for 10 shirts, 20 pairs of stockings, 10 guns, 30 bars of lead, 30 pounds of powder, 12 coats, 2 pieces duffil, 30 kettles, 50 hatchets, 25 hoes and a number of knives and awls. Two years later the Indians complained that the terms of sale had not been complied with, and the Dutch were compelled to add more trinkets when the island was finally delivered to Thomas Lovelace and Mathias Nichols.

Tea, coffee and chocolate came in due time to the new country, tea being brought in 1701. The early way of preparing it was strange indeed. The leaves were boiled, the liquid thrown out, and the leaves buttered and salted and eaten — with none too much relish. Tea was also made from herbs — a custom carried on for many years. A license had to be obtained to sell tea; in England it was sold in apothecary shops.

Coffee-drinking was a general habit first acquired at the time of the Revolution, although coffee had been served as early as 1670. Chocolate, spelled chockolett, appeared in the colonies in 1697, coming from South America and the West Indies. Mills were invented to grind this bean or seed, as were mills for grinding coffee; such mills were boxes of wood, with an iron holder, blades and crank.

A USEFUL ARTICLE WAS THIS CHESTNUT OR COFFEE BEAN ROASTER WHICH WAS MADE TO FIT INTO THE STOVE HOLE FOR HEATING.

V

Everyday Life Throughout the Year

LIFE IN THE early kitchens was one of ceaseless activity. There was no time of the year when there was any let-up of the duties that confronted the pioneers in the new land. Making their homes, their furnishings, their equipment and clothing, foraging for food, planting and harvesting, preparing whatever was eaten, facing a relentless Nature — never was mankind more brave and fearless than in the years of the seventeenth century.

The four seasons of the year came and went, and each one brought its demands, its special tasks and its pleasures. To each belonged such occupations as were characteristic of the season; Nature offers to man little monotony.

Spring came on the calendar with the equinox on March 21; but spring actually came when the sap began to flow back in the trees and the maples glistened in the sunshine with tiny icicles of sap which formed after the cold, frosty nights at the end of February; when the pussy willows broke open their tight coverings and buds began to swell; when the robins and bluebirds returned to herald another breaking-up of winter. It was then that man as well as beasts and birds recognized a force that urged them on in preparation for another year of living.

Spring was a busy time in the house and outdoors, for both women folk and men folk, and the children too. In New England, a most important task of spring, and one also of fes-

tivity, was that of sap gathering. Hardly a family but had a grove of maple trees and the sap afforded a substantial income, giving sugar, syrup and sugar-molasses for the table and often for barterng. If the maple trees were at some distance from the house, a miniature village was set up in the grove. There was a sugarhouse with a place for fire and kettles, and there was a shack or two where the family and all those engaged in the undertaking might eat and sleep. Often the kettles were swung outdoors in a clearing, suspended on a stick held by two low-spreading trees. Many kettles were in operation at one time, four or even five, depending on the amount of sap that was gathered; there were lean years and there were years when an abundance came from the trees.

The Indians taught the white man how to tap trees, for the maple tree had been a source for sap to the red men for countless generations. The Indians used stone spouts, after boring holes in the tree, and the sap flowed into hollowed wooden troughs. Those first troughs were hollowed-out logs. The white man used spouts or spiles made of sumac twigs with the pith burned out, and under the spile there was a wooden bucket to catch the dripping sap. The later tin spiles were an improvement over those of wood, for they had a lip which held the bucket. The sap bucket has a short protruding stave with a hole in it by which it was hung.

If there was a large number of trees, and

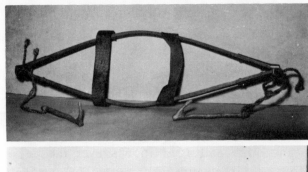

spout, watch the full buckets being poured into tubs and follow the lumbering oxen to the sugarhouse. Fortunate are the children today who have such an experience in their lives, keeping watch of the buckets on the trees, lending a hand in driving the horses carrying the tubs, and watching the unloading at the sugarhouse.

The sap was stirred in the kettles with long wooden spoons, but little stirring was needed, because in boiling it broke the grain as it formed. The women folk were there to lend a

THE SHOULDER YOKES SHOWN ABOVE WERE SOMETIMES KNOWN AS INDIAN YOKES BECAUSE THEY WERE FOUND AMONG THE CAPE COD INDIANS. THE TWO SAP BUCKETS, AT THE RIGHT, WERE CARRIED ON SHOULDER YOKES. *Museum of A. B. Wells.* THE FUNNEL AT EXTREME RIGHT WAS USED FOR POURING SAP INTO BARRELS.

if they were widely scattered, two oxen were hitched to a scoot that drew the tubs from tree to tree, guided by a man with a stick. Another man emptied the full sap buckets into the tubs. A scoot was a low platform or runners that carried three or four tubs. The oxen plodded along with the filled tubs to the sugarhouse or to the swinging kettles, and there the sap was boiled.

Some preferred to gather the sap without the oxen and scoots, using a shoulder yoke instead. This was of wood, shaped to fit the shoulders and neck, and at the ends of it hung two leather thongs, to which were fastened two wooden hooks on which the buckets were carried. By this means a sap carrier was also used; this being a tub having two short staves with holes through which a stick was thrust. The stick could be fastened on the hooks of the shoulder yoke, balancing the carrier in an even position.

It was a great lark for the children to join the older folks and watch the sap pour from the

THE LARGE MAPLE SUGAR TUB BELOW STANDS THREE FEET HIGH. AT THE BOTTOM IS A LONG-HANDLED MAPLE SUGAR STIRRER.

hand, for there must be constant watching so that the sap did not burn nor the fires go out; it was a day-and-night task until done, lasting three or four successive days.

The first syrup was poured into boxes with partitions, each section having a design in the bottom, not unlike those in the butter prints. When the sugar hardened, the partitions were removed and the cakes could be separated into squares or oblongs, as the case might be. Each cake was then wrapped, and they were packed in tubs to be kept until they were taken to market. Later, molds were of tin and made in fancy shapes, such as hearts, stars, tiny flowers and figures, or round shapes with corrugated edges. Each year saw more and more decoration used in the product.

The second run of sap made a darker syrup, and this went into soft sugar and was stored away in barrels, with a bunghole at the bottom. As the sugar set, a sugar molasses formed, and this was drawn out whenever it was needed for cooking or for serving with buckwheat cakes and the like. This sugar molasses was used before molasses from the sugar cane found its way to the tables of the early settlers, but even then it was enjoyed greatly by the young folks and considered superior to anything else.

When the last of the sugar had been made into cakes or poured into barrels, an evening of gaiety was planned — a sugaring-off party — when neighbors from far and near came to the camp through the snow, in pungs, to join those working in the grove. Singing and games enlivened the evening, and between times they poured syrup on snow and ate the delicious, chewy substance. It was simple pleasure, but it made an indelible impression on young and old. Such an evening came as the climax to the days of hard work at sap gathering. The full moon added luster to the snow, while the fires burned under the kettles.

Another late winter and early spring task was cutting timber, followed by sprucing up the place and building fences. Cutting trees was begun in February at the wane of the moon, and all the men in the community joined in helping clear the forest, stripping the trees of bark, and taking the logs to the river banks on scoots, so that they might be rolled into the water when the ice broke and the streams were clear. Such uniting of communities in work was called "change work," and each family was ready to go to any other and assist in whatever the task might be. More hands made not only a quicker job but made much merriment, which lightened the heaviest task. A chopping bee was not uncommon, and food and drinks were generously set forth, and games indulged in.

Trees for splint and hoop poles were cut later in the spring when the sap was flowing freely, and these were hauled into the yard to be left to dry or weather until time for using them. The splint was used for making cheese baskets, winnowing baskets and sieves, apple-drying baskets, eel traps, vinegar funnels and general utility baskets; while the hoops were for barrels, tubs and buckets.

It might be that a newly married couple planned a house, or perhaps a new barn was needed. All hands lent themselves to the house-raising or barn-raising, and it literally was a raising, as has been described earlier in the book. The timber for each side of the framework was placed flat on the ground in position; sill, summer and girts, fastened together with wooden pegs, or later with hand-wrought nails. Then by means of ropes, pulleys and tackling, each side was raised into position and fastened to the adjoining side, and thus all was ready for the rafters for the roof. The laying of the ridge pole was the climax, and a bottle of rum was broken over the ridge pole, as a christening. The whole affair was jubilant, and there was much to eat and drink. As many as forty or fifty men handled the job, and it entailed considerable risk.

Fences came in for their share of attention. Instead of cattle and poultry being fenced in, as was the custom later, fences were built around the house, yard, garden and tilled fields to protect them from the roaming creatures. Geese roamed at will, as did swine, the latter being cared for by hog-reeves, men who saw that the

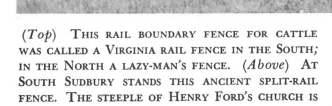

(*Top*) THIS RAIL BOUNDARY FENCE FOR CATTLE WAS CALLED A VIRGINIA RAIL FENCE IN THE SOUTH; IN THE NORTH A LAZY-MAN'S FENCE. (*Above*) AT SOUTH SUDBURY STANDS THIS ANCIENT SPLIT-RAIL FENCE. THE STEEPLE OF HENRY FORD'S CHURCH IS SEEN IN THE DISTANCE. (*Below*) WHERE STONES WERE ABUNDANT, WALLS, BEING MORE DURABLE, TOOK THE PLACE OF RAIL FENCES. A SINGLE RAIL ADDITION SOMETIMES WAS BUILT ON A LOW WALL TO ADD HEIGHT. GATES WERE USUALLY MADE OF RAILS.

hogs were branded, had rings in their nose and did no damage to crops. Geese were often yoked two by two, and there was always an old goose that kept the flock more or less together.

Each man had his cattle pastured on the "common," the central pasture in the town, common to all. The cattle were branded with a mark of the owner, burnt on with a branding iron; or marks were cut in the ear — the term "ear mark" was derived from this method of marking. The owner had to supply and build twenty feet of fence for every cow he had pastured, and this section of fence he had to keep in repair. He also fenced his own cornfields, a law being passed as early as 1633 that cornfields should be protected by fences.

A man who inspected such fences was called a "fence-viewer," and he reported any work that needed to be done. There was also a "line-viewer," who inspected dividing lines and allotted shares or sections of fences, and saw to it that they were kept in repair. Hay fields were also watched over, the men having that responsibility being called "hay wards." Thus all tilled land was carefully protected, for crops were most important in those lean years.

Fences are and always have been an interesting part of the landscape. Different sections of the country have different types of fences; moreover, as the years have passed, changes have come about in the types of fences. The first was the log stockade built for protection against the Indians. Then came a boundary fence for cattle, made of rails. It was called a Virginian rail fence in the South; in the North it was called lazy man's fence. Rails were laid zigzag on the ground, each end lying across the end of the adjoining rail. A second rail was laid above the first, again held in place by the ends of the adjoining rail. As many rails were laid as were needed for the height of the fence. Such a fence was an artistic addition, as shown by the illustration. This has also been called a snake fence, because of the way it winds along the ground.

For another type, two posts were driven into the ground and crossed, and in the crotch rested the ends of the adjoining rails. This was called a post-and-rail fence. These two types of fences could be put up without any fastenings.

In the South, there is the so-called snake fence of saplings; out West there was the split-rail fence which became famous through Abraham Lincoln. The idea for this had been brought by a pioneer from the East, from the region near Boston. This split-rail fence was made by driving into the ground posts in which holes had been made to hold the rails of the fence. In some sections, there were fences made from tree stumps.

Board fences came after the sawmill was common, and when wood was still abundant. The later type of fence in the nineteenth century was made of wire, after wood became too scarce for such lavish use.

The appearance of stone walls coincided with the plowing of new fields. For it was from the fields that stones were turned up, and were thus ready at hand to make the walls that are so common in certain sections of the country, especially in New England. The fences of wooden rails deteriorated all too quickly, and stones made a much stronger as well as a more orderly-looking wall. When only a few stones were turned up, a low wall was built; and on top was made a rail-fence addition the height of a single rail, supported by posts. But stone walls have been built as high as four or five feet and as wide as a team of horses, one such wall being located on the outskirts of Worcester, Massachusetts.

All the work on fences and walls had to be finished by April, for it was then that the live stock was put out to graze, having been housed all winter in barns and shelters.

There was hardly a house but needed some repairing in the spring after the long, severe winter. A new roof, a new chimney, a new jog or ell to be added, a new shed for more room, or a new lean-to or wing for an addition to the family. In New England, houses were frequently added to, rather than entirely new houses being built, which accounts for some old houses appearing to be two or even three houses joined together, in the form of a T, an L or a square

U. Each part had its own chimney and fireplace for heat and for cooking.

As the days grew warmer and the sun climbed higher in the sky, the gardens called for attention. Plowing and sowing took much time, and many acres were under tillage in the colonies within a few years. Corn ranked the highest in demand, with wheat, rye, oats and barley also in use. Parsnips, carrots, squash, pumpkins, peas, turnips, cabbage and melons were planted. Potatoes were a long time being accepted, but eventually they became a common vegetable. What the settlers had known in the old country was tried out in the new land, and there was a variety for the table before another generation had grown up.

While the men were busy with the outside chores, the women were equally busy inside the house. Spring was housecleaning time for them, and cleaning house in a thorough manner was characteristic of the early generations. It was all hard work. And springtime meant a fresh coat of paint in the rooms, for paint was used inside the house, though outside painting was not done for several generations. There were gay colors that went into the pantry, on walls and floor, on buckets, boxes and tubs. Pumpkin yellow, turkey red and wagon-wheel blue were popular names of the colors.

Though the early settlers in their first homes sanded the floors, it was not many years before floors were painted. In the nineteenth century, a spattered floor was popular, made by first painting the floor with a solid color and then spattering many colors over the entire floor, making specks of color.

Paint was made from the clay in the soil, mixed with whites of eggs, whey or skim milk. The three colors of clay were red, yellow and gray. The clay deposits were often called paint mines. To obtain various colors, dyes were made from barks, berries and flowers, with the gray clay used as a base.

Black came from charcoal; brown and yellow from the bark of the red oak and hickory; gray from berries and barks; mahogany color from the liquid made by boiling walnuts; buff from chestnuts; madder from a plant whose root gave a deeper color than the red clay; green from the berries of dogwood, skunk cabbage, wintergreen and other shrubs; and blue from the indigo plant, first imported from India and later grown in the new land.

A task for which the women had been preparing in the winter was that of making soap. Fats taken from meat when butchering had been saved and "tried out," and the clean maple and birch ashes from the fireplace and the ash oven had been saved.

Making the lye was the first step. Before the days of staved barrels, the sour-gum tree was used for barrels because it became hollow as it aged and could easily be made into a barrel-like receptacle. A board floor was put into it, with holes that would act as a drain. This log barrel was placed on a stone in which had been chiseled a groove, the stone being larger than the size of the barrel. At the front edge a tub was placed. Into the barrel went a layer of straw, then lime, then a layer of ashes, and this was repeated until the barrel was two-thirds full. Then rain water was poured in. For three days, water was added, and it soaked through the substance in the barrel, and trickled out slowly into the groove and down into the tub. When it reached the tub it was lye. If of the proper strength, an egg or a potato would float in it.

Alice Morse Earle has quoted from an old-time receipt: "The great Difficulty in making Soap come is the want of Judgement of the Strength of the Lye. If your Lye will bear up an Egg or a Potato so you can see a piece of the Surface as big as a ninepence, it is just strong enough."

Sometimes there were two or three circular drains on the stone, for as many barrels; or two separate stones with drains might be used. These stones were called lye stones or leach stones, and the process of obtaining the alkali from the ashes was called leaching. The old stones make attractive doorstones today, but they are not common.

The lye was mixed with the grease in a big iron kettle over a fire and stirred with a sassafras stick. This wood was used presumably because of its slight odor, which would cut that of the grease. Usually the kettle for soap-making was hung in the yard. After much stirring, the soap would "come." It was a clean, jelly-like substance.

It took about six bushels of ashes and twenty-four pounds of grease to make a barrel of soap, which would be a day's work. The soap was kept in barrels in the shed or down cellar, and scooped out as needed with a flat-sided scoop made from a block of wood. Those scoops, white and cracked, show how lye eats into wood.

THE HOME-MADE SOAP OF THE COLONISTS WAS KEPT IN BARRELS AND SCOOPED OUT AS NEEDED WITH FLAT-SIDED SCOOPS MADE FROM BLOCKS OF WOOD. HARD SOAP WAS NOT COMMON UNTIL THE MIDDLE OF THE SEVENTEENTH CENTURY.

Hard soap from bayberries was sometimes made, but not until the middle of the seventeenth century was hard soap at all common. In many families, soap was made twice a year, rather than in one batch of many barrels. Ashes accumulated rapidly and there was always a quantity of animal grease. It was a difficult job to make soap, and the women tackled it before housecleaning, so as to have the ashes and the grease out of the way.

Washing was another spring task, done when the winds of March and April would blow through the linens as they lay on the bushes or hung on hemp lines. Records vary as to the number of times a year washing was done, but it is safe to say that it was seasonal before it was monthly. The great amount of linens with which a daughter was dowered was not to show wealth, but to provide a large enough quantity to last from one infrequent washing to the next.

The first method of washing clothes was to beat them on stones at the banks of streams. It must have been a wooden club that was used as a beater. In some foreign countries, clothes were placed in a huge receptacle filled with water, and young boys were engaged to tread on them. Walking back and forth, the boys' feet acted as paddles to beat and mangle the clothes.

In this country clothes were washed in those early years as they had been done in the old countries, the people of each nationality following the customs of their ancestors. One can imagine that a washtub was among the first things fashioned to ease the labor of the housewife. The larger the family, the larger was the wash and the larger the tub. It stood out in the dooryard on a log bench, that sturdy bench made from a broad slab taken from the side of a tree, the top smoothed and the bottom left in the rough with the bark on. Water for the washing was carried from the pond or brook and heated in the iron kettle outdoors, or perhaps indoors on the crane in the fireplace.

An early list of possessions tells of linen sheets, pillow cases and bolster cases, napkins and "board cloths" or table cloths; while later one reads of aprons, shirts for men, chemises, petticoats and underwear, and always the linen and lace caps.

An English poet of the late sixteenth century, Thomas Tusser, wrote about the time of washing:

Dry sun, dry wind,
Safe bind, safe find.

Go wash well, saith summer, with sun I will dry;
Go wring well, saith winter, with wind so shall I.
To trust without heed is to venture a joint,
Give tale and take count is a housewifely point.

One of the first implements for washing in the tub was the dolly. This was a wooden affair used to stir and mangle the clothes in the tub. It measured about two feet long and seven inches in diameter at the large end, where there were four deep grooves that caught the clothes as the dolly was twisted about in the tub. It was shaped like a wild man's huge club, and was made of oak, ash or maple, with a handle running through the upper end, by which it was grasped. It must have been a difficult job for the housewife to wield the dolly in a tub filled with clothes, water and soft-soap jelly.

Another implement which seems to have been less violent in its functioning was the pounder. This had a long broom-stick handle, with a heavy head at the end. Every man fashioned his own pounder and every man had his own ideas about how to make one. The principle was to have a suction in the head, and there had to be weight. One in the author's collection is made of lignum vitae, the heaviest of woods, having an outside cup in which are holes, and an inner round knob. Others were made of maple blocks, with holes bored on all four sides, making suction. One is a heavy block of wood, painted the old blue, and has four deep grooves cut in to catch and turn the clothes.

One less thoughtful man — possibly a youth — made his pounder of four pieces of wood, nailed to a long handle. The four pieces are shaped like wedges of pie and within the cup which they form is a long tongue, which is the end of the pole handle. No nailed slabs of wood could resist the constant wear and the effect of water; and today this pounder not only looks, but is, worn-out and useless, having served its full time.

These pounders were used in a barrel called a pounding barrel. It would seem an easier task to fill the barrel with clothes, water and a generous amount of soft-soap jelly and work the pounder up and down, than to churn the dolly in a tub of clothes.

Strangest of all washing implements is an iron contraption that has a crank with a handle. The body of it holds a foot-long stick that can be raised or lowered by means of a screw, which adjusts it in relation to the clothes in the tub. The crank turns a cogwheel, and that in turn sets in motion a large tin suction cup, five inches in diameter, which works up and down. The cup has a frame across it to prevent the clothes

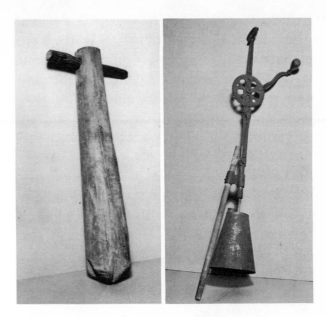

THE WOODEN DOLLY PIN WAS USED TO STIR AND BEAT CLOTHES IN THE TUB. (*Above right*) HERE IS A SUCTION CUP, CONTROLLED BY A CRANK, THAT WORKED UP AND DOWN IN A TUB OF CLOTHES. (*Below*) A FAVORITE WASHING IMPLEMENT WAS A LONG BROOM-STICK EQUIPPED WITH A HEAVY HEAD. THIS ONE WAS MADE WITH FOUR SIDES NAILED TO A HANDLE WHICH HAD A TONGUE AT THE END.

from being sucked in, and there is a vent at the top of the cup for the intake of air. It is indeed an odd contrivance, the production of some genius who attempted to put it on the market with "patent pending." But it seems as if it must be the only one of its kind.

The first washboard was called a scrubbing stick, and was a narrow slab of wood, corrugated on one side, with a handle cut at the end by which it was held while the scrubbing was being done with the other hand. The corrugations are cut on a slant to allow the water to run away from the working hand; it was made definitely for a right-handed person.

Other washboards show ingenious minds. There is one with a set of narrow corrugations on one side and coarse ones on the other; one made of spools set up and down, like the posts on a spool-bed; another of spools set horizontally; one made with heavy rollers set into curved sides, and with a back board which prevented the water from coming out onto the worker. The spools and rollers turned as they were used, so that no one side was subjected constantly to wear — which made the washboard last longer.

A strange device of wood has a corrugated attachment fastened to the main board which has rollers. The attachment was used to rub the clothes against the main board as it rested in the tub. Pegs and peg holes are at the back, so that the board could be adjusted to the height of the tub.

It is interesting to note here that one of the first patented washers, put out in 1869, was an arrangement of rollers. The upper part consisted of a four-inch roller cut with fine, rounded corrugations, set in a frame and turned by an iron crank. Below this were four separate rollers that revolved when the upper roller turned them. The affair had the appearance of a wringer, but the idea was to thrust the clothes between the rollers and turn the crank back and forth, not full circle, which motion mangled the clothes. When sufficiently mangled, the clothes were cranked through, and out into the tub. The machine was called "The Little Washer," and in purchasing it the buyer had to purchase also a tub, which had iron clamps attached to hold the apparatus.

Washing machines followed on the heels of the early homemade devices. Undoubtedly the first washing machines were made at home — a tub set on four legs, a cover, a four-winged paddle turned by a crank, and a hole low in a stave, with a spigot where the water might flow out to empty the tub. Or there might be four upright rods set into four arms, making a frame that was turned by a crank.

Factories for wooden ware made their appearance at the beginning of the nineteenth century, and more and more elaborate wooden contrivances for the house were produced. When washing machines came into general production, they were made on the same principle as the forerunners — the dolly, the pounder and the suction cup — with paddles and arms that mangled and stirred the clothes. These patented washers continued to be made of wood until metal usurped the place of wood. Metal was more durable, and eventually replaced wood entirely.

Without doubt, the washing was first hung on bushes or laid on the grass to whiten in the sun as it dried. Then hemp rope appeared, and a hemp line was strung from tree to tree. At this time clothespins came into existence. They were whittled by hand from a stick of maple, beech or birch, and were about eight inches long. They were shaped on a lathe and finished by hand with an auger and a jackknife. A hole was bored for the slit and this was finished with a

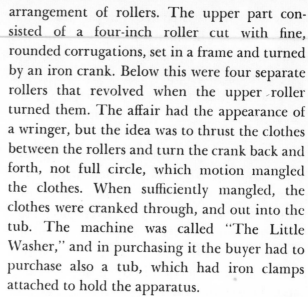

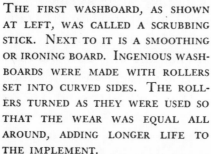

THE FIRST WASHBOARD, AS SHOWN AT LEFT, WAS CALLED A SCRUBBING STICK. NEXT TO IT IS A SMOOTHING OR IRONING BOARD. INGENIOUS WASHBOARDS WERE MADE WITH ROLLERS SET INTO CURVED SIDES. THE ROLLERS TURNED AS THEY WERE USED SO THAT THE WEAR WAS EQUAL ALL AROUND, ADDING LONGER LIFE TO THE IMPLEMENT.

knife. Beautifully shaped and polished, the pins are examples of perfect handwork. Some clothespins never saw a lathe — they were fashioned entirely by hand, and no two are alike. In due time factory-made pins replaced the hand-made ones.

In the days when there were no stoves, but only fireplaces, ironing was called smoothing, and the ironing board was a smoothing board. Such a board was not unlike the first scrubbing stick, and can easily be confused with one. The smoothing board is from eighteen to twenty inches long, three to five inches wide and a full inch thick. One side has corrugations, more rounded than those of the scrubbing stick. On some boards there is a handle, on the upper side at one end, made in one piece with the board, and a knob set in at the other. Some boards have ornaments on them, such as scrolls, hearts, flowers, birds, hex marks or initials. There is such a smoothing board, credited to the year 1770, that has no corrugations on the under side. The handle of this board is in the form of a mermaid, suggesting that the board may have been made on a whaling vessel, on a trip from far places.

Many smoothing boards have no handle and no knob on the upper side, but a handle that protrudes at one end, and some sort of attachment at the other end that the hand could grasp. One board has a raised extension; while another one had an extension nailed to the edge — but this came off in time and was lost. One has two much worn notches at the end, in which the fingers rested as the hand gripped the board. These boards with protruding handle and end rests for the hand are slightly curved, so that the hand did not drag on the table as the implement was used. They show much ingenuity in the way in which they were made.

A search by the author for a smoothing stick covered several years. Then, not only was

THIS DEVICE OF WOOD WAS EQUIPPED WITH A CORRUGATED ATTACHMENT, THE ROLLERS OF WHICH RUBBED THE CLOTHES AGAINST THE STATIONERY MAIN WASHBOARD AS IT RESTED IN THE TUB.

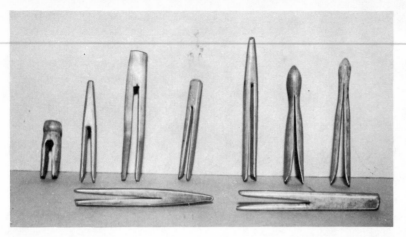

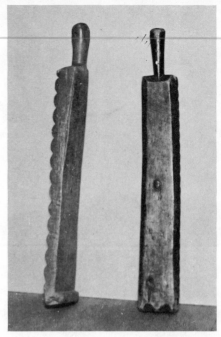

EARLY CLOTHESPINS WERE WHITTLED BY HAND, SHAPED ON A LATHE, AND HAND-FINISHED WITH A JACKKNIFE; SOME WERE FASHIONED ENTIRELY BY HAND. SMOOTHING BOARDS, AS SEEN AT THE RIGHT, WERE FROM EIGHTEEN TO TWENTY INCHES LONG WITH CORRUGATIONS ON ONE SIDE AND HANDLES AT THE END.

one found, but a second, shorter one came to light. The longer one, measuring twenty inches, has a middle diameter of about two inches, and tapers at the end to half an inch. Giving consideration to this shape one realizes that when a sheet is folded to make four thicknesses, the folds and hems are thicker than the middle section. Thus the tapered ends afforded room for this thickness. The shorter stick, of similar shape, must have been used for narrow sheets, pillow cases and towels.

The process of smoothing had been used in the old country, and the custom continued in this country. The sheet was folded and rolled onto the stick before it was perfectly dry, and placed on the table. The smoothing board puhed it back and forth, the roller catching in the corrugations of the board.

In the old country, and in warmer sections in the new country, a washhouse was considered a necessary addition to a home. Here were kept the utensils and implements for washing and smoothing, and later for ironing. A fireplace was built into an end wall, and beside it was a built-in set kettle. This was built in a framework of bricks, with a place for fire below, where wood was burned to heat the water. It amazes one to learn that the process of washing, drying and smoothing or ironing took a whole week, or sometimes two weeks, depending on how many

sheets and other homespun linens were used in the family. But it must be remembered that washing was done only twice a year, or perhaps once a season.

In Sweden, clothes were bleached with a liquid called lute, obtained from boiling birch ashes in water. This custom was followed in many sections in this country. The iron kettle hanging on the crane in the fireplace was filled with birch ashes and water, and this was brought to a boil. After the clothes had been washed they were wrung and put into another tub. This second tub had holes in the bottom bored by a gimlet, or else had a spigot, by means of which the water could be drawn off. Then the lute, obtained from boiling the birch ashes, and containing lye, was poured over the clothes, running through them and out at the bottom. This was repeated several times until the clothes were beautifully bleached.

Rain water is another agent for bleaching clothes, and every home had a rain barrel at the end of the spout, to catch water on a rainy day. It has been said that hanging clothes out on a line on a rainy day whitens them, the rain water acting as a bleach.

The history of ironing is an interesting one. Following the wooden smoothing board came implements of iron, created by a blacksmith.

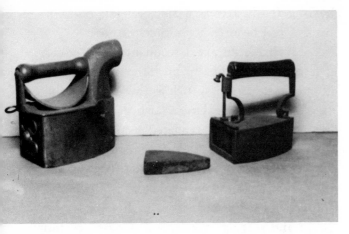

BOX IRONS, WHICH APPEARED IN THE LATE NINETEENTH CENTURY, WERE MINIATURE CHARCOAL STOVES COMPLETE WITH FIREBOX AND CHIMNEY, ILLUSTRATED BY THE EXAMPLE AT THE LEFT. THE IRON AT THE RIGHT WAS HEATED BY THE SLUG (*foreground*) WHICH, IN TURN, WAS HEATED IN THE EMBERS. TWO SLUGS WERE USED AND HEATED IN ROTATION IN ORDER TO KEEP THE IRON HOT.

They were first used in Europe, and were called box irons. The box was pointed, had hand-wrought uprights and a wooden handle, and a trap door that lifted with an arm.

Within the box of one such iron, the floor is set with delicate curlicues of iron so that the heat might circulate. With this iron, slugs were used, of the same shape as the bottom of the iron. These were heated on a stove, or in the embers of a fireplace, and when hot they were placed in the box, through the trap door. Thus

the box was heated, and it was always clean for ironing. There are several types of box irons.

The first all-iron implements were called sadirons, for sad in this use means heavy. These were hand-wrought, and what appear to be the earliest have a handle coming from the center in one shaft. Later ones were cast, and the handle comes from two points; these were made in sets of different weights and were numbered and often stamped with the company's name.

With these sadirons, or flatirons, there were rests on which the irons stood. They are of many patterns and are most ornamental. They have sometimes been called trivets; but a trivet, according to Webster, is "a stand to hold a kettle or similar vessel near the fire; a tripod." Correctly, they are called flatiron stands.

An early iron is one made partly of soapstone. The bottom is iron, and on this an upper part of soap-stone is fastened with a screw and nut, attached to the socket of the handle. There is a wooden handle — wooden handles did not absorb the heat as rapidly as did those of iron. A second type of soapstone iron is one that is pointed at both ends; this was used for pressing rather than for plain ironing.

A box iron that appeared in the late nineteenth century held charcoal. It is a miniature stove, and has a smoke stack and an opening at the back with a slide cover for a draft. The top,

THE FIRST ALL-METAL IRONS WERE CALLED SADIRONS, SAD AT THAT TIME MEANING HEAVY. THE SADIRON AT THE RIGHT IS PARTLY MADE OF SOAPSTONE. THE HOLDER, CALLED A FLATIRON STAND, RESTED ON THE STOVE.

including the stack, is removable, so that the charcoal could be put into the box. This was far from being satisfactory, for the charcoal was dirty and often blew out through the draft vent onto the clothes.

Still other irons were the later ones with a removable handle. There was a slot in the top of the iron into which a spring catch in the handle fitted. Several irons could be in use, with one handle for them all, which could be transferred from an iron that had cooled to a hot iron. These are the last of the family of irons before the present day; they were considered a great improvement over the earlier ones.

Tailors and manteaumakers had their irons, made definitely for their work. This type of iron was called a goose, from the fact that the handle resembled the neck of a goose. The common one was hand-wrought. It was long and narrow, with a pointed nose and a square back. These had a twisted handle, a mark of better hand-wrought articles. Smaller irons, in the shape of goose, had pointed ends, for finer work.

An unusual goose is one shaped like the hoof of a horse, with round nose and square back, and extremely heavy. This goose has on it the initials, N Y, supposedly the maker's mark. Another tailor's goose, a small iron pointed at both ends, has a removable handle. Still another, made of brass, is long and slender.

In the early years, tailors and manteau makers went from house to house doing family work — in the manner of cobblers and coopers. It would seem that it was too much to expect a tailor to take along a goose, so one surmises that individual families had a goose or two.

With the box irons, appeared various irons for ironing or pressing bonnets and small articles. These were called tally irons, a shortening of the term, Italian irons. They were listed in the seventeenth century, and were also called goffering irons, sometimes spelled gauffering. They were made with a standard, and a long tubular section at the top of the standard. Some stands had two tubes, or barrels, while others had only one. These held a poker-like iron that was heated in the embers. The poker was thrust into the barrel red-hot, and a second poker was heating in the embers while the other one was being used. A bonnet or a mobcap was laid onto the barrel and moved about as it was smoothed or ironed by the heat. The heating irons or pokers have been confused with the iron flip-dog or toddy iron, both having a long, slender head on a shank or handle. Those for heating toddy are, as a rule, longer, but both irons could be used for either purpose.

Fluting irons are descendants of the goffering iron, in another form. They were used to flute or crimp ruffles, such as those on clothing, on curtains, or on valances for beds. These irons were made in two corrugated sections, one section fitting into the other. There are some that have two hinged parts that would lock together when in use. These have no mark of the maker, and appear to be very old.

Some fluting irons have a base on four short legs, with a part that is curved so that it could rock back and forth. A brass one comes to light occasionally; such ones came from across the water at an early date. One rocker, labeled "THE CHARMER," is made of iron with steel corrugations. Another type has a corrugated plate or standard, with a second part made as a roller, to be pushed back and forth in the process of fluting. One of this type bears the date 1866, and the instruction to heat the base. When there were two separate parts to a fluting iron, the base was heated, the cloth to be fluted laid on it, and the second part pressed down to make the fluting.

Very small irons are found in various types, one especially attractive one being in the shape of a duck. These small irons have holders on which they rest. The question arises whether such small irons were models that were shown as being representative of what the factories were making, or were toy irons for children to use on doll clothes.

Curling irons might perhaps be classed with other irons. They could hardly have appeared in this country until the nineteenth century, for the women folk had little time to spend to make themselves beautiful. One type of old curling

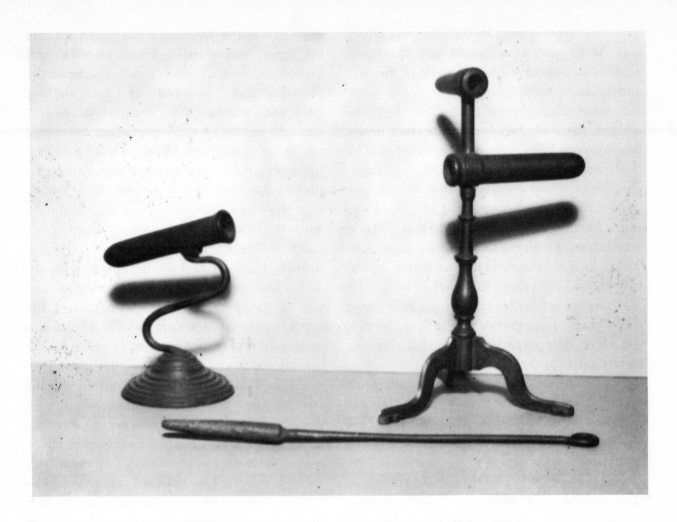

GOUFFERING IRONS, USED FOR PRESSING BONNETS AND SMALL ARTICLES, WERE HEATED BY THE IRON ROD SEEN IN THE FOREGROUND OF THE PICTURE. SMALL PIECES TO BE IRONED WERE PLACED ON THE TUBULAR HOLDER AFTER THE HOLDER HAD BEEN HEATED WITH THE ROD.

iron was like a pair of pincers, with a half-cylindrical head at each end. These were made in more than one size. They were used to press into shape the ringlets on a woman's forehead — "beau-catchers."

Crimping irons, too, were like pincers, and the first were wrought by the blacksmith, delicate arms fitting one within the other, with curved tips on the handle. There was a later type with two cylindrical ends on one arm and three on the other. When heated, these pressed or crimped the hair and made it wavy. Perhaps the strangest implement for crimping the hair is a pair of crimping boards made of wood, about five inches wide and eight inches long. The corrugations fit one within the other. The boards

were heated on top of the stove, and then a lock of hair was placed between them — the result, a wavy lock. A pair in the museum must have been left too long on the stove, for it is black from scorching.

In the early days as soon as the washing and ironing were out of the way, plans were made for dipping candles. Not all housewives could make their own candles, but called on a chandler, one who made and sold candles. Candles were made either in the spring or in the fall, depending on how much grease had accumulated. Tallow was obtained from the suet or fat of sheep mostly, sometimes from that of cows, although not much of this was available for some years after the founding of the colonies, for in the early years the animals were not killed, being more necessary alive. At first, tallow was made from bear's grease and the fat of the deer and moose.

Some time previous to the day of candle-making, the wicks had been made from hemp, tow or cotton, or even from milkweed fiber. The cords were cut twice the length of the candle, and doubled and twisted deftly to make one slender cord, with a loop at the end. A candle rod, a slender, smooth stick of birch or hickory, was thrust through the loops of five, six or eight wicks. Two chairs were placed back to back, and two rods about twenty-four inches long were placed on top of the backs. On these rods rested six of eight of the shorter candle rods, holding the wicks, thus preparing for making thirty or forty candles in the lot.

The nursery rhyme about the candle stick sprung from this part of the candle dipping:—

> *Jack be nimble, Jack be quick,*
> *Jack jump over the candle stick.*

The modern use of candle stick, meaning candle holder, has given the idea of Jack jumping over a candle in a candle holder. The poem was written about those candle sticks resting on chairs.

The fat or suet was scalded in water and skimmed off; and scalded and skimmed a second time. This layer of pure tallow, free from any particles, was taken out with a tallow scoop. The scoop had a round head of tin with a half-cylindrical piece attached in which were holes; thus the scoop was used as a skimmer. In many of the pantry tools that we see, there is a distinction between those for a right-handed person and those for a left-handed person. The illustration of the two tallow scoops shows the two types.

The tallow was put into boiling water in two huge kettles over the fire, ready for the oper-ation of dipping. One kettle was swung out into the room, and a rod holding the wicks was dipped and set back onto the rods resting on the chair backs. A second rod was dipped and put back, and so on for the six or eight rods. By that time the first set of wicks was sufficiently cooled to dip again. Dipping continued until each candle was of the proper size, the tallow being replenished in the kettle as needed.

Sometimes the tallow was poured into a tub and the dipping was done in that, but the tallow hardened quickly and had to be reheated. Dipping could not be done too rapidly, and it took much skill to handle the rods and dip the wicks. If the tallow hardened too quickly, the candles were brittle. The candle rods were often suspended on chairs in an adjoining room, away from the heat.

When cooled, the candles were slid off the rods, any imperfections smoothed and the loop cut off. The candles were stored in long tin boxes called candle boxes, or in wooden boxes, and were set away in the dark to keep them from turning yellow. Two hundred candles could be made by the housewife in one day, with the help of some other member of the family — perhaps the grandmother or a daughter, or a neighbor. Skill in candle-making was a matter of pride with women of early days.

Candles were used both in the home and in church services. There are countless candle holders in existence. Those used in the home are in pewter, brass, tin, iron and glass. And there were holders of wood to stand on the floor or hang from the mantel, with one or two arms to hold a candle. These screwed on a spiral standard to adjust the light to the necessary point. In churches there were chandeliers of

IN CANDLE-MAKING THE TALLOW WAS DRAWN OFF WITH ROUND TIN TALLOW SCOOPS HALF COVERED BY A PERFORATED TOP. AS CAN BE SEEN IN THE PHOTOGRAPH, THESE WERE MADE BOTH RIGHT AND LEFT-HANDED AND WITH SHORT AND LONG HANDLES.

(*Above*) CANDLE BOXES OF TIN WITH HINGED COVERS WERE IN COMMON USE FOR HOLDING CANDLES. (*Right*) TIN CANDLE MOLDS WERE USUALLY FITTED WITH HANDLES. THE LARGE SINGLE MOLDS IN THE PICTURE WERE USED FOR MAKING ALTAR CANDLES; THE MOLD AT THE LEFT MADE TWO DOZEN CANDLES AT A TIME.

wood, iron or tin, called candle-beams, which held several candles. There were sconces of all types. A rare holder found by the author had once swung in the cabin of a whaling vessel. This has four arms with holders and four convex reflectors, and is filled with sand to give it weight — a necessary factor at sea.

Tinder boxes, with a candle set in the cover, were also in use. In the box was a piece of flint, a striker and a cover to snuff out the blaze started in a bit of rags. Miners had a special candle holder which could be hung on a cap or jabbed into a crevice. These were used in both salt mines and coal mines.

There were candle snuffers to extinguish the flame, and pick-wicks to keep the wick burning brighter. The snuffers were sometimes conical in shape, and were made of tin and wood; but a scissors-like affair with a box head was more easily used. Those used for chandeliers were in the form of a long copper arm with a snuffer at the end. A pick-wick had a metal pin point in a copper handle set into a copper standard. These are rare today.

After a period of dipping candles by hand, tin molds were made that held two, four, six, eight, ten, twelve or twenty-four candles — or even a single candle. The molds were placed upside down, the tip at the bottom. The tow wicking was twisted over a piece of wire, the number of wicks depending on the number of molds to be filled. The piece of wicking was run down each mold, the end protruding through the tip, and the wire rested across the top, holding the wick in the center of each mold. Then the tal-

low or wax was poured in, filling the mold. When thoroughly hardened, the candles could be pulled out by lifting the wire — animal tallow never stuck to the sides of the molds. The wires were pulled out, any imperfection in the candles was attended to, and the loops cut from the end.

TWO TINDER BOXES, ONE DISASSEMBLED AND ONE PUT TOGETHER READY FOR USE AS A CANDLE HOLDER. NOTE FLINT, STRIKER, AND COVER THAT WAS USED TO SMUDGE A FIRE.

The common variety of molds, made of tin, had a handle at the side by which the mold was held when being filled. Some molds were built into box frames, an unusual one having pewter molds in a frame on standards. Single molds were not the usual thing; the large single mold pictured was used when making candles for the church altar.

THIS RARE TIN CANDLE HOLDER WAS ONCE USED TO LIGHT THE CABIN OF A WHALING SHIP. THE UPRIGHT CYLINDER WAS FILLED WITH SAND TO GIVE THE LAMP ADDED STABILITY.

Wax taken from bees was occasionally used for candle-making, but a favorite wax was taken from the bayberry. These berries have such small amounts of wax on them that it takes thousands of berries to provide enough wax for one candle. The burning wax sends out a fragrance which is most pleasing; moreover, a bayberry candle does not bend, and burns more slowly than a tallow one. The English called the bush a bayberry bush, or a candleberry bush; the Swedes called it a tallow shrub. These bushes grew in profusion, and were of such importance that laws were passed concerning the gathering of the berries. Soap and sealing wax also were made from the wax of the bayberry, which was considered especially desirable for soap because of its fragrance.

One of the earliest methods of obtaining light was by the use of pine knots from the pitch pine. These knots were used by the Indians and by early settlers in the various colonies, both indoors and outdoors. The colonists called the wood candlewood. Accounts of that period have often mentioned the pine knot on the hearth, used to give light for reading.

Outdoors, the pine knot was carried in an iron frame called a cresset. The sides were some-what similar in appearance to the ribs of an animal, and they were fastened to a long center rod. This extended at the end, making a pole which could be stuck into the ground. When cressets were used in a boat, the long end was fastened into the gunwale. Thus at night time the pine knot threw out its flickering light for hunting or fishing. Cressets were hand-wrought, and were made in various designs, according to the ideas of the individual makers.

Small cressets were used at the hearth to hold the pine knot for light. These are cages or frames made of iron bands a foot or more in height, and used standing upright. The cooper had an iron cage to hold fire for charring the inside of a cask and making the staves flexible.

Rushlights were another early means of lighting. Rushes growing in marshes by the sea were stripped of their outer bark, and then dipped in tallow or other grease — preferably in mutton tallow — after which they were spread to harden. They were used like candles, being placed in rushlight holders. These were made of wrought iron, and were somewhat like pincers fastened to a base. A rushlight was about fifteen inches long, and would last half an hour, being moved along in the jaws of the holder as it burned.

In primitive lamps, from as early as Bible times, tallow, grease and oil from animals and fish were burned. As the years went on, petro-

USED FOR OUT-OF-DOORS LIGHTING, THIS CRESSET WAS FASHIONED TO HOLD BURNING PINE KNOTS.

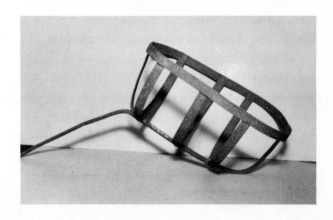

leum was discovered, kerosene and camphine were developed, and the history of lighting continued through its many chapters. For the various illuminating substances, there were holders of pewter, wood, china, glass, tin and brass.

One important spring job for the women was that of plucking the geese, and a mattress filled with goose feathers was considered a luxury. In the first lean years the stuffing was beech leaves, straw, cattails, or corn shucks shredded with a hetchel. Any of these made a rather hard bed on which to lie, but one consolation was the fact that new stuffing could always be obtained.

The goose was considered dumb, like the ostrich; when once the head was covered, the bird was helpless. At the time of plucking, a black cloth was tied over the eyes. Then the head was held between the knees and the plucking was done with both hands, with speed and skill. The down flew everywhere, and the pickers had to be well covered in doing the work. A splint goose basket, shaped like a bottle with a small neck, was invented early. Into this the head of the goose was thrust.

Plucking wild geese appears to have been done as early as the fourth century, and twice a year, springtime and harvest time. In the American colonies, it was customary to do it

three or four times a year. Quills for pens were pulled but once a year, for this killed the bird if done more often.

In some sections flocks of geese were owned by almost every family, and the flocks ran freely about town. They caused much disturbance with their clacking, but not much was done about controlling them. Sometimes a goose yoke was used, linking two together, which made it more difficult for them to stray off, or to get over boundaries. The flesh of geese and later that of ducks was considered a delicacy.

Another important event of springtime in those early days was the coming of the peddler. When the peddlers packed their goods and set forth to sell, what a conglomeration were in those packs! At first the peddler rode a horse, but by the eighteenth century it was a horse and wagon that started out over the rough and narrow roads. There were spinning wheels, clock reels and flax reels in the wagon. There were clocks that were not in a case, but were made to hang on the wall; such a clock was called a wag-on-the-wall. There were guns; boots for the men, women and children; hats for the men and bonnets for the women; and dry goods such as cloth, trimmings, buttons, needles and thread. There was furniture, too, for many men did not

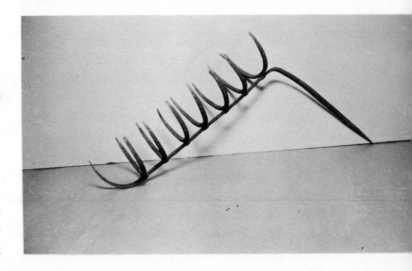

SPLINTERED BIRCH BROOMS HAD A VARIETY OF USES IN THE AMERICAN COLONIES. THE SMALL ONE SHOWN ABOVE WAS FOR BEATING EGGS WHILE THE OTHERS WERE EMPLOYED IN SWEEPING OVENS AND FOR CLEANING KETTLES.

make their own and were only too glad to have some brought by the peddler who came in the spring.

In exchange for the goods from the peddler, a night's lodging might be given, with the attendant meals; and butter, cheese and extra food was taken away by him as he journeyed on to the next town. Rags were given, too, in exchange for paper which he might have with him. Perhaps the weather was such that he remained more than one night, and a family never failed to offer hospitality. Something, too, which the peddler carried with him, though not in his pack, was gossip, and he had plenty of that as he went from house to house. He was the carrier of news, both good and bad, from one family to another, and each family in its turn was eager to hear what he had to say.

A task which boys were required to do, and which they could do well, was to make birch brooms. There was hardly a boy but had a jack-knife that he had earned by hard work, for whittling was almost the first thing a boy craved to do. Springtime saw the boys going after yellow birch saplings, or in some sections young blue beech, for these woods have a long, unbroken grain, the birch more so than the beech. The brooms they made were called Indian birch brooms, for the Indians had made them, and they taught the white boys how to make them.

A slender sapling was cut, making a stick about six feet long. First it was stripped of its bark, and at the distance of about a foot from one end a ring was cut around the stick. Then this end was slivered, in very fine splinters. The center, or core, was taken out, and the splinters tied at the top with a stout piece of tow string, from the coarse part of hemp.

Next, beginning about a foot above the splintered part, more splinters were made, and these were turned down over the ones already tied. Then the whole lot was tied, and instead of using tow again, the fastening was sometimes made by braiding three strands of splinters, twisting the braid around and tying it securely. The braid of splinters would not last as long as the hem tie, but it looked neater.

The rest of the stick, to be used as the handle of the broom, was made smooth, sometimes being polished with a piece of glass, and a hole was cut near the end by which the broom could be hung. Sometimes the work of making a broom took the greater part of three evenings, and the compensation was small, for the brooms sold for six cents each at the village store. The boys might trudge as much as ten miles to the village, carrying the brooms on their backs — coming home seemed shorter, with the money jingling in their pockets. Girls could whittle, too, and they sold their brooms for trinkets and ribbons. As many as a hundred brooms came and went in the village store each season.

The splintered birch broom was made in several sizes, and no two brooms were ever alike. One long floor broom was for the barn floor — this was made from a large sapling; a short broom was used in washing iron kettles and sweeping the floor of the bake oven before the loaves of bread were put in. Some of these brooms were made with only the first cutting of splinters, with no second set covering them. Such brooms were more bristly, as the illustration shows.

A broom not commonly found today is the one for whisking eggs or cream. This was tiny, not more than five inches long. The one in the author's museum is finished with a braid of splinters. A more sanitary whisker was the one made from a six-inch stick, with gashes cut around the stick for two inches or more at the end. The cut sections protruded sharply, and when the stick was twirled between the hands they caught the egg or cream and beat it, or whisked it.

A broom such as witches are pictured riding was made by fastening birch or hemlock twigs to a handle — more often hemlock, with its close-growing branches. The branches were tied on with a hemp cord. Brooms of this sort were much more sturdy than the splintered broom of birch. They were called besoms in olden times. In Isaiah xiv, 23, it says: "I will sweep it with the besom of destruction."

When spring was well along, with warm days and new green grass, the cattle were put out to pasture. This meant being taken to the "common," the ground that everyone in the community shared for their cows, sheep or goats.

In the spring the sheep were heavy with wool, and it was then that the shearing was done. The sheep were driven into a pool of water or a nearby stream and washed for shearing. It was not an easy task to shear sheep, and unless it was done by those accustomed to the work, the animals were sometimes nipped and injured. After losing their heavy coats of wool, the sheep were

SHEEP OWNED BY THE EARLY SETTLERS WERE MARKED BY BRANDING BLOCKS THAT HAD BEEN DIPPED IN A TARRY SUBSTANCE AND WERE THEN PRESSED INTO THE WOOL.

done up with a covering of straw or corn shucks to prevent them from catching cold.

In Massachusetts alone, there were 3,000 sheep by 1644, and there was considerable restraint against using the animals for anything but wool, so great was the need of clothing. In Pennsylvania and New York state also, sheep were bred in large numbers, and here, too, the wool industry kept pace with the demand for clothing.

After the wool was taken from the sheep, it was washed a second time and cleaned of branding marks. The brands were put on sheep with a wooden block dipped in a tarry substance, and this had to be carefully removed from the wool. Picked, pulled and separated, and smelling fresh and clean, the wool was then laid on the grass to dry.

The wool was combed with two wool-combs; these were shaped like a letter T, at the top of which were thirty steel teeth, ten to eighteen inches long. The combs were heated, the wool was placed on one comb and combed with the other. The process took out the waste which was called noil; this was spun into a coarse yarn.

Carding was the next step. The hand carders used resemble the currycombs for horses; they are oblong boards filled with short wire teeth and having a handle; a pair was used in the work. Before the carding began, the wool was greased with melted swine grease, so that it might work more easily; three pounds of grease went into ten pounds of wool. A bit of wool then was placed on one carder and combed and brushed with the second carder, a peculiar motion being needed to work the wool from one to the other. The last motion was to roll the wool, then fluffy and light, making a roll the length of the carder and one inch in width. These rolls were laid in a basket ready for the spinning wheel. For many years all this work was done at home; but later, after mills were set up, carding was sometimes done at a mill, to relieve the women folk of this task.

Dyeing wool has been one of the arts practiced from earliest times; and many were the sources that supplied the colors the colonial settlers used for dyeing their wool. Sometimes the wool was dyed before it was carded, but it could be dyed better in skeins. Flowers, herbs, leaves and roots gave the colors: the indigo plant, madder, cochineal, logwood, red oak, maple, hickory, goldenrod, pokeberry, violets, sassafras, balsam, field sorrel, walnuts, charcoal and many combinations were used.

Spinning the wool for the loom was a pleasant task, and one that was often done by the grandmother of the family. The spinning wheel was turned by a wooden wheel driver, called a "speed boy," not unlike a toddy stick in appearance. It has been said that a woman spinning six skeins of yarn a day walked twenty miles as she stepped back and forth, holding the delicate thread of wool as it wound itself onto the spindle. The spindle of wool was next wound off into skeins with a clock reel, which ticked off the length of the wool into the skeins. Or a hand reel was held in the hand and wound by hand; this type of wheel was also called a niddy-noddy. And there were small spinning wheels called quilling wheels, which wound the quills or spools to be used for the woof of the weaving.

The skeins were sometimes dyed at this point rather than before the wool was spun — no rigid rules were followed in seasonal tasks, and no two families did these things in exactly the same way. After the skeins were wound, they were put away in baskets or chests, or in drawers, to await the winter, when the loom was brought out from the corner and the weaving was begun. But if an emergency arose, and cloth needed for a garment, the weaving was done at the time.

In Nantucket, sheep raising became a great industry and the time of sheep shearing was made a festive occasion. Families helped each other — a custom called change work — and often an entire village helped with the task. After the shearing was finished and the sheep were back in the pasture, a feast was laid out on the table — pies, cakes, tarts, cookies, gingerbread and cider, both fermented and unfermented. This was a gathering of much merriment, which was anticipated every spring.

Spring slipped into summer. The foliage grew heavy, the grass long, the days lengthened, with sultry heat and thunderstorms, and with some delightful cool days for good measure. Gardens were tended, haying was a job that called for many hands; and by midsummer, vegetables were on the table in abundance and the barns were filled with hay for the winter ahead.

Repairing the house, inside and outside, might be done at any season, but the work was most often done in between the regular jobs of the summer. A man had to be handy with his tools to keep up with the work.

In midsummer the women turned to cheese-making. The first step was making ren-

Two useful devices employed in the making of wool yarn. (*Below left*) A clock reel was used to wind the yarn while the quilling wheel (*below right*) wound the bobbins.

Niddy noddys, shown below, also came in handy when there was yarn to be wound after spinning.

AN OLD SPINNING WHEEL IN A CORNER AT THE PUTNAM HOUSE IN RUTLAND, MASSACHUSETTS, STANDS UNDER AN EARLY PRINT OF GEORGE WASHINGTON.

net. For this, the stomach of a young unweaned calf was used. This was washed and turned, and washed again and put away in a strong brine. When well salted, it was taken out and put away in jars or bags called cheeseleps, to stay until it was to be used.

The day the cheese was to be made, cut-up pieces of this rennet were soaked in water, and the liquid thus produced was put into the milk to curdle it, and the mixture was stirred with wooden paddles. It was then placed in cheesecloth, either in a wooden cheese drainer or a splint cheese basket, resting on a rack or ladder over a tub, and the curds separated from the whey. The whey was fed to the pigs, mixed with corn meal. The stiff curds were broken up with a long wooden knife called a curd knife, or put through a box having a roller with wooden teeth. This mass was then put into a wooden bowl and salted, and worked until ready for the press.

The old cheese presses show much inge-

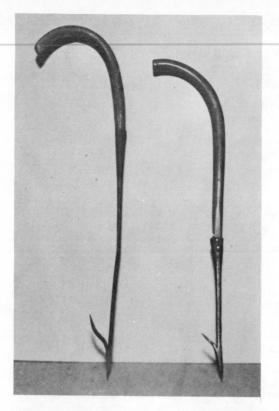

THESE HAY PULLERS, HAVING A HEAD OF IRON AND A SHAPED WOODEN HANDLE, WERE USED TO PULL HAY FROM THE MOWS AND TO MAKE SURE THAT THE HAYCOCKS IN THE FIELDS WERE PROPERLY STACKED WITH NO BRIERS.

nuity; many of them were made at home. Some presses held only one cheese, while others held two or three. Some were operated by wooden screws; others had weights and pulleys. The worked curds were placed in a hoop lined with cheese cloth, which rested on the small board floor of the press. A cover called a foller fitted inside the hoop, and the function of the screw or weights was to press this cover down and press out the liquid. A groove in the floor board carried off the liquid, which ran down into a bucket underneath. The next morning the cheese was taken out and the cloth removed. Pared and smoothed, it was wrapped with a narrow strip of cheese cloth that covered the sides only, lapping over several inches; the top and bottom were left exposed and buttered. Then the cakes were placed in a cheese closet.

The cheese closet was made with four or five shelves and had a frame door onto which cheesecloth was tacked. The cloth allowed air

in the closet and at the same time kept out the much dreaded cheese fly. It was the use of this thin gauze cloth on the cheese closet that gave it the name of cheesecloth. The cakes of cheese were placed on the shelves and each day were buttered on the exposed top and bottom; and each day one or more new cheeses were added to the shelves. It took three weeks for cheese to be cured, or to ripen, and then it was ready for market or for family consumption.

Cottage cheese was made by leaving the curds unpressed, and it was salted and buttered to suit the taste. Dutch cheese was made by crumbling the cottage-cheese mixture, salting and buttering it and working in chopped sage. This was formed into pats and set away to ripen. The Dutch were great users of cheese and owned large herds of cows. Cheese was often varied by adding spinach water or water from the pigweed for flavor.

Next to butter, cheese was the most necessary commodity in the home, and it was used for many generations for barter; calico, needles, trinkets, spices, shingles, clapboards, wood from the sawmill and meal from the grist mill — all

CHEESE DRAINERS, SUCH AS THE ONE BELOW, WERE USED WHEN SEPARATING CURDS FROM WHEY AFTER THE CURDLED MIXTURE HAD BEEN PLACED IN CHEESE-CLOTH.

these might be obtained in exchange. It was not uncommon to pay the minister and also cowherds or other keepers with butter and cheese.

Another cheese, named for its shape, was the pineapple cheese. It seems to have originated among the Dutch who settled in New York state, and was called Holland pineapple cheese. The making of this type of cheese spread to Goshen, Connecticut, which became a great cheese center in the last quarter of the eighteenth century. In 1802, a mammoth cheese, weighing 1,450 pounds, was sent to President Jefferson. The amount of cheese carried to market in Goshen in a year was 270,000 pounds, bringing an income of almost $24,000 to the farmers.

The pineapple cheese was made from the milk of cattle that grazed in pastures from May to November. The curds were first colored with annatto, a coloring matter made from the pulp surrounding the seeds of a tree growing in the tropics. This dye was also used in butter, following the use of carrot juice.

The curds were pressed in wooden block molds, which were hollowed out to shape the curds into a pineapple form. Next they were

THIS CHEESE PRESS CAN STILL BE SEEN IN THE RUFUS PUTNAM HOUSE. IT IS BUT ONE MODEL AMONG MANY, THE VARIETY OF WHICH WAS PRACTICALLY LIMITLESS.

THIS LARGE CHEESE DRAINER HAS WINDSOR SLATS AND WAS PLACED ON A RACK OVER A TUB WHEN A BAG OF CURDS WAS DRAINED.

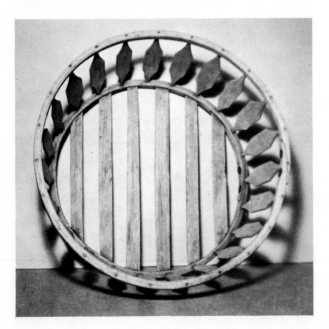

put into conical-shaped bags, which were made of coarse twine, with a mesh woven so as to impress on the cheese a print resembling the print of a pineapple. The bag, with the cheese in it, was dipped in hot water and then hung up to dry. After the cheese had dried and ripened sufficiently, it was taken out and covered with a coat of varnish, to protect it in any climate.*

Together with wool, flax and hemp were all important in the home, flax ranking first for its use in clothing and for its seed, while hemp was used for such things as bags, ropes and cording. A field or patch of flax and one of hemp were planted early in the spring, and by late June or July, the stalks of both plants were ready to be picked, roots and all being pulled from the ground. In Virginia, wild flax grew in profusion.

An account of the processes of handling flax has been given very fully by Alice Morse Earle in *Home Life in Colonial Days*. Briefly, the stalks were left to dry several days in the sun

* Information from the writings of William L. Warren in *The Chronicle*, Albany, N. Y.

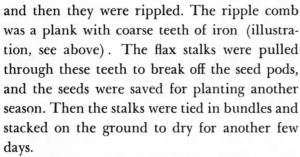

CONSIDERABLE SKILL WAS REQUIRED OF THE WOMAN
WHO OPERATED THE SMALL FLAX WHEEL. NOTE
HETCHEL FOR SEPARATING FLAX FIBERS ON THE
FLOOR BESIDE WHEEL.

and then they were rippled. The ripple comb
was a plank with coarse teeth of iron (illustration, see above). The flax stalks were pulled
through these teeth to break off the seed pods,
and the seeds were saved for planting another
season. Then the stalks were tied in bundles and
stacked on the ground to dry for another few
days.

The hemp was not rippled, but was stacked
along with the flax. Then the stalks, called
"bates," were placed in a brook or stream of running water, where a box had been built to hold
them. They were placed with one layer crossing
upon another, and were weighted down with
stones. The stalks rotted in four or five days and
then were taken out, the leaves pulled off, and
the poor stalks discarded. Well cleaned, they
were tied in bundles, and were ready for use.

"Breaking" the flax and the hemp was the
next step, this being done by the men, for it required a good deal of strength. The flax brake
separated the fibers and removed the woody center from the sheathing, for it was this center that
was used in the final spinning. The brake consists of two sets of heavy wooden blades built
into two massive uprights. These are hinged at

one end and fit one within the other. A heavy
mallet is attached to the upper set of blades.
The stalks were placed on the lower set of blades
and the blow given by the upper set and the
weight of the mallet mashed and broke the
stalks.

By this time, the fibers were well cleaned
and free of the bark, and they were again made
into bundles. The last operation was putting
the fibers through the hetchel, also called the
hatchel, hackel or heckle. This was a narrow
board with a block of long headless spikes,
set close together. As the fibers were drawn
through, being slightly wet, the long fibers were
separated from the short ones and they formed
in continuous threads. The short threads, called
tows or hards, were coarse. This operation was
repeated many times until the long broken
fibers were ready for spinning, the short ones for
coarser work. The entire process, from rippling
in the fields until the last pulling through the
hetchel, counted up to twenty manipulations;
and even then the most careful work lay ahead,
when the fibers were wrapped around the spindle for weaving.

The job of making the skeins ready for
weaving fell to the women; this required skill
and dexterity. The threads were spun from the

fiber on a small flax wheel and wound on bobbins. When all the bobbins were filled, the thread was wound off into knots and skeins on the clock reel, which ticked off forty strands to a knot. The clock reel had a clocklike device with notched wheels arranged to snap when the knot was completed. The strand was then tied to the next, until there were forty knots, twenty of these making a skein. A day's work amounted to two skeins of linen thread.

The last process of preparing the skeins before weaving was to bleach them. The skeins were washed in a flowing brook and bleached with ashes and hot water in a tub called a "bricking-tub"; the operation was called "bricking." This had to be repeated several times before the skeins were thoroughly bleached. A last rinse was made in clear water, where the skeins remained a week.

Flax was grown for seeds as well as for thread used in weaving fine linens, for there was a great demand for flax seed, for linseed oil, used in making paint. The seeds were also used in poultices for sores and inflammation.

In late summer the kitchen was a busy place with the preserving of fruits and berries, and with pickling and spicing. Wild berries were found in profusion, and later, when fruit trees were planted and orchards flourished, the tables of the colonists held a great variety of sweetmeats, and crocks of earthenware were filled with delicious concoctions.

When autumn came, it was time for the harvesting. And there was much to be harvested — corn and the other grains, and all the vegetables. September's moon was called the harvest moon, and it shone on the many preparations for winter. The mild spell in November known as Indian summer was the time when the Indians laid away their stores of food for winter, and the white man in the new land did likewise.

The grain was cut in the fields, spread on the barn floor and threshed, or — as it was called colloquially — thrashed. The threshing was done with flails, which were long handles of wood with leather thongs at the end. Or sometimes a short stick was fastened to the handle with

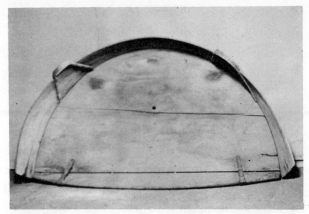

THIS LARGE WOODEN WINNOWER (*top*) AND WINNOWING BASKETS WERE TWO OF OUR FOREFATHERS' MOST IMPORTANT HARVESTING TOOLS. BY MEANS OF THEM THE GRAIN WAS SEPARATED FROM THE CHAFF, A JOB THAT IS NOW DONE BY THRESHING MACHINE.

straps of leather or iron rings, playing free as the flail was swung to beat the grain. Two men worked together, one pacing the floor in one direction and the other in the opposite direction. In Pennsylvania, threshing floors were built with narrow spaces between the boards, through which the kernels fell as they were threshed from the stalks.

Gathering the broken stalks into large splint baskets, called winnowing baskets, the men stood at the barn door and tossed the grain in the baskets, letting the chaff blow out and leaving the grain in the bottom. These baskets, were large, oval-shaped ones, somewhat like a big scoop, the length of a man's arm. Then the grain was sifted in a winnowing sieve, which had a fine splint bottom, and the kernels were caught in buckets. The sieve was then struck against the barn floor to free it of any remaining chaff, and another lot was sifted.

Before the day of mills, grinding was done by hand in mortars with a pestle. The earliest mortar of primitive man was a stone hollowed out by Nature, or a piece of a tree trunk; while the pestle was a club-shaped stone, or perhaps a pestle of wood in the shape of an L. A pestle of this shape afforded more of a blow than did a straight limb. Savages conceived the idea of fastening the pestle to the end of a branch or to a small sapling, which held the weight of the pestle. The pestle was pulled down to pound the grain in the mortar and then the branch sprang back, lifting the pestle. This method was used in many sections by the white man for he, too, saw the advantage of the free branch holding the weight of the pestle. It is said that many isolated families signaled to each other by pestle and mortar, and that they could call for aid or send friendly messages for a long distance. Sailors are said to have known when they were nearing the coast by hearing the thud of a pestle, carried far in the wind.

There was always a stone pestle lying handy, and small hand mortars and pestles were used in the kitchen for pounding and mashing such commodities as sugar, salt, herbs and spices. Maple, cherry, lignum vitae and maple burl were the woods used; often the pestle had an iron tip to give it more weight. The Indians had a tall wooden mortar with a shallow cavity in which they pounded corn that had been first parboiled in water; this made a samp or coarse hominy.

Mills for grinding the grain by hand were called querns, from an old Anglo-Saxon word meaning corn. Two circular grooved stones were placed together and turned by hand. But before long windmills were set up, copied after those in Holland. The Indians were frightened by the moving arms, believing that evil spirits were moving them. Then came the water mills, for nearly every town had been located by the water, both because of transportation and for water power. These mills were called grist mills, and millers were appointed by the officers of the town, being allowed as a salary one-sixth of the meal which they ground.

The first windmill in America was set up in Virginia in 1621. Massachusetts had one in 1631, and in 1635 a grist mill was running in Ipswich. In Virginia, by 1649, there were five water mills, four windmills and a great number of horse mills and hand mills. The numbers increased rapidly as grain became abundant, and in every section, before many years, mills were running to grind the meal for the tables of the colonies.

After the harvest, the remaining ears of corn were stored away, the shocks stacked and left standing in the fields, with golden pumpkins lying on the ground all about. Some of the ears were stored for seed for another year, the husks turned back and braided in the manner called "tracing." These were hung in the shed, the shed chamber or "up attic" to await the time for shelling; or they might be hung from the beams in the barn. Some of the ears were kept for popcorn, and after a few months of drying they were taken down and shelled, and a jolly evening it was when the corn was popped over the embers in the big fireplace on a winter's night.

The first primitive way of shelling corn was to rub the ears against the edge of a shovel resting on a tub. Various shellers were conceived to alleviate the work, one being made of two planks filled with headless nails, which were fastened to an easel. Barrels were used that had floors of grating, or floor boards with holes in them, allowing the kernels to drop through. The different types of shellers all had the same aim — to make lighter work out of a hard job.

Corn shucks had many uses, the most important of which was as stuffing for mattresses; for this purpose the shucks were shredded through the hetchel. Then there were braided mats made from the shucks, a type very useful for the back entry or at the kitchen door. Even though they wore out quickly and had to be replaced frequently, they were good dirt catchers and saved wear and tear of the floor.

The large tree mortars were made from gumtree wood whenever possible, for the tree grows hollow as it ages and a mortar cut from a piece of the trunk needed less time spent on it. The bark was stripped off and the sides smoothed and a board put in for a bottom.

When crisp October weather came and the full moon hung in the sky — October's moon was called the hunter's moon — plans were made for a corn-husking. This was one of the merriest gatherings of the year for both young and old. It was hoped that there would be plenty of red ears, for the man or boy who found one was privileged to exchange a kiss with his sweetheart — and if he did not have a sweetheart, this was a good time to show a girl that he would like to court her. After the great piles were shucked, a feast was waiting in the house, with tables loaded with good things to eat, and plenty of cider. In later days, a fiddler was added to the gathering, and in the evening square dances were enjoyed in the barn until a late hour, with light from lanterns hanging on the wall, and the moonlight streaming onto the barn floor. Such gatherings, for work and fun together, enriched the lives of the communities.

Besides having a grove of maples, every family living in the country soon had an apple orchard planted. The trees were brought from across the water and after a few years of being carefully tended, the fruit was abundant. There was hardly anything in the early colonies that yielded as much in the way of food as an apple tree. Cider, boiled cider, applesauce, apple butter, apples for pies, apples for puddings, apples to bake, and dried apples to be used later — all these provided nourishment and variety. And of course there were the dishes of apples set out to eat raw, especially in the long winter evenings, in front of the fireplace.

Cider was first made by crushing the apples in a mortar and straining the pulp. Then various inventions appeared in some form of hand press, similar to a cheese press. Instead of the hoop which held the curds, a round or square box of wood or tin, with holes in the sides, held the mass of ground apples, which was called pomace. A heavy screw of wood or iron pressed down on a board cover, forcing out the juice

HOW CIDER USED TO BE MADE: APPLES WERE CRUSHED INTO A MASH CALLED POMACE BY THIS HAND-OPERATED ROLLER CRANKED BY TWO MEN.

into a channel in the floor board and down into a bucket below. A grinder for apples had metal teeth, instead of wooden ones, as the curd breakers had; but the grinders for apples or grapes are often confused with the ones for curds.

Large apple presses were first turned by hand, then by horse power and later by water power, passing through the same evolution as did grain mills.* The apples were first crushed by revolving wooden cylinders, and the pomace was allowed to lie overnight. The following

* From correspondence of N. R. Ewans, Camden, New Jersey.

THE POMACE WAS THEN PUT INTO A COARSE FIBER BAG AND PLACED IN A HAND PRESS. WHEN PRESSURE WAS APPLIED, THE JUICE FLOWED OUT OF THE PRESS INTO THE LARGE TUB BELOW.

135

THIS IS A KIND OF GRINDER THAT WAS FREQUENT-
LY USED FOR CRUSHING APPLES BEFORE THE POM-
ACE WAS PLACED IN THE HAND PRESS. STEEL PINS
ON THE ROLLER HELPED SPEED UP THE PROCESS.

the straw kept out the ants and allowed some air to get in to help ferment the cider. It was a man's pride to possess many barrels of cider and to mention them in his will, for cider was considered a necessity, and it was rated with other supplies for the table. Thirty barrels in the cellar was not at all unusual, part of this being converted into cider-brandy, called winkum.

Boiled cider applesauce and apple butter

morning, it was ready for the press. At the bottom of the press was a grooved platform, and on this was placed a layer of straw. Next went a layer of pomace, shoveled with wooden shovels. Then another layer of straw was placed crosswise of the first layer, then more pomace, and so on until the mass was about three feet high. A board was placed on top for a cover. Screws pressed down blocks that pressed on the cover, flattening the mass. As the pomace squeezed out at the sides, it was cut down with a long knife that had a blade fully eighteen inches long and four inches wide. Such a knife, called a "cutting-down knife," is sometimes confused with a frow, which was a cleaving tool with a handle set at right angles to the blade, and was used with a mallet; but the knife for apple pomace shows that it was never struck and mutilated by the heavy wooden mallet.

The pomace cut off was added to the mass in the press, and a second pressing was made; sometimes this was repeated several times before all the juice was extracted. The mass of pomace was called a "cheese," for it was not unlike a cheese of curds.

The juice ran down into the channels of the platform and out into buckets or tubs below. It was then poured into casks by means of a bucket funnel, actually a small tub with a wooden funnel projecting about six inches. The casks were sealed at the bunghole with deftly twisted straw, in lieu of a wooden stopper, for

THIS HAND PRESS FOR MAKING CIDER IS EIGHTEEN INCHES HIGH AND WAS DESIGNED SO THAT IT COULD ALSO BE USED FOR MAKING WINE FROM GRAPES OR ELDERBERRIES. THE PRESSING BLOCK, OFTEN CALLED A FOLLER, CAN BE SEEN ON THE FLOOR IN FRONT OF THE PRESS.

were made in large quantities; the Shakers made and sold both commercially. The apples were cooked in a copper or brass kettle, which measured three and four feet in diameter. Iron kettles were not used, for iron turned the apples black. In Pennsylvania, the kettles were hung over fires in the open, or in the washhouse. Long stirrers from Pennsylvania show what the size of those kettles must have been, and give an idea

TWO GADGETS FORMERLY IN COMMON USE FOR PAR
ING APPLES. THE BASE OF THE ONE ABOVE WAS
USED AS A SEAT WITH THE PARER IN FRONT. THE
THREE-LEGGED PARER AT THE RIGHT WAS INGEN-
IOUSLY CONSTRUCTED SO THAT THE SLANTED BACK
LEG KEEPS IT IN BALANCE.

of the amount of sauce and butter made each fall. One such stirrer in the author's collection measures nine feet long, and has a head fastened at right angles that is nearly two feet long. In the head, which is paddle-shape, holes were bored in the broad tip, through which the sauce or butter poured as the stirrer was pushed back and forth to keep the mass from sticking to the bottom of the kettle. A deep groove is worn in the handle, two feet back from the head, show-ing where it rested on the edge of the kettle. This mark also shows that the diameter of the kettle must have been approximately three feet.

Another apple-butter scoop, possibly of Shaker origin, is one with a double-barrel han-dle that was used on end, one hand pressing down on the top of the handle. The scoop itself measures more than twelve inches. Still another scoop has a handle three feet long, with a snubbed nose. All such wooden ware was made as the need arose, for each task called for a dif-ferent tool, which could be fashioned by the men folk.

Applesauce was made with both sweet and sour apples, cooked with cider, molasses, maple molasses or apple molasses. Apple butter was made with cored and quartered apples and cider, sweetened with sugar and cinnamon, the rule reading, "ten gallons cider, three pecks ap-ples cored and quartered, ten pounds sugar and five ounces of cinnamon." Slow cooking for five or six hours made a delicious syrupy paste. But the fire was hot enough under the kettles that straw was placed on the bottom of the kettle to keep the apple butter or apple sauce from burn-

ing. Both the sauce and the butter were put away in the larder or buttery to freeze and to be used in the long winter.

Puddings made from apples were called by various names, which differed according to the locality. Apple slump, apple mose and apple crowdy all sound interesting. Apple pies put in an appearance at an early date and were found on every table, sometimes three times a day. The custom of eating pie for breakfast continued for a long time. Wooden pie crimpers vouch for the fact that pies came before metal tools appeared in the kitchen; and some of the old rolling pins with two rollers are museum pieces.

Apple-paring bees were another festive oc-casion among the women folk. Neighbors joined in helping each other and were rewarded with a jolly time topped off by good things to eat and drink. There were many kinds of apple parers, from the one that screwed to the table to one on four legs, like a bench. The worker could sit on this one. Other parers were placed on the table or in the lap. Wheels and belts worked some of them, but there was always a crank and a wooden knife with a metal blade which pared the apple. Later inventions of iron were nu-merous, the first one being patented by Moses Coates in 1803.

Dried apples were found in every home, and they were on the shelves of every country store until late in the nineteenth century. There were two ways of cutting the apples for drying: one to pare and quarter them and string the

137

quarters; the other to pare, core and slice them. It was a matter of taste. The quarters were strung on heavy black thread, two yards to a needleful, and these strings were hung to dry on racks, over hooks, or on frames made especially for this purpose.

For drying the sliced apples, there were many kinds of racks and baskets, which were set out in the sun or suspended from the ceiling over the heat of the fire. One large basket of splint was made to rest on the window sill, half in and half out, and as the apples were dried the basket was rotated and all the slices were sunned. One beautiful rack of splint was made in cobweb shape, and was intended to hang by its center from the ceiling, the heat spinning it around and drying the slices. Other racks were made of thin slabs of wood, or were in the form of a frame of slats. From Pennsylvania comes a flat fruit-drying platter of wood.

After drying, the slices were packed away in large wooden boxes, to be used in the winter months for pies and puddings. Dried apples were also used for barter. Pumpkins were cut and dried in much the same way as apples; this was another idea passed on by the Indians.

The Shakers carried on extensively the work of drying apples. The brethren operated the parers and the sisters cored the apples. They had a drying house with heat on the lower floor and bins on the second floor to hold the slices.

As an important part of the preparation for winter there was, of course, much preserving and pickling. Great amounts of spices were im-

ported for the sole purpose of being used in preserving; jars and crocks were filled with concoctions so rich that they did not need to be sealed. "The housewives pickled samphire, a plant growing on the seacoast, the herb fennel, purple cabbage, nasturtium-buds, green walnuts, lemons, radish pods, barberries, elderberries, parsley, mushrooms, asparagus and many kinds of fruit and fish. They candied fruit and nuts, made many marmalades and quiddanies from quinces, and a vast number of wines and cordials." * These were the sweets which supplied the table.

Cranberries grew on Cape Cod, and blueberries abounded throughout the land. Each section had its own characteristic ways of preserving and pickling, all alike taking care that there would be an abundant supply for the winter months.

Butchering was done in November, and this was a disagreeable job. In the early years, it was only the hogs that were killed, for cows and sheep were more valuable alive.

Hogs were scalded in great wooden barrels called hogsheads, block and tackle, or pulleys and ropes being used. The hide was scraped of bristles with an iron tool, and someone had the bright idea of using the bottom of an iron candle holder for this purpose. Thus this type of holder acquired the name of "hog-scraper" candle holder.

It has been said that everything about the hog could be used except the squeal. The meat was smoked in smoke ovens and packed away in oats to freeze, or it was powdered in powdering tubs, which was a method of preserving it in salt. And the Dutch crown, the circular iron frame with many hooks set in around the edge, hung from the ceiling in the larder, holding a dozen or more hams, as well as other meat to be frozen. There was little craving for fresh meat then, as in the twentieth century.

The intestines of the hog were used in making sausages, and the sausage gun, a tin tube with a snout and a wooden plunger, was one of the common kitchen implements. Sometimes

FLAT SPLINT BASKETS OF THIS TYPE WERE DEVELOPED FOR DRYING SLICED APPLES. THEY WERE EITHER PLACED IN THE SUN OR EXPOSED TO THE HEAT OF THE FIREPLACE SO THAT THE MOISTURE WAS REMOVED AND THE APPLES LEFT READY FOR STORAGE.

* Alice Morse Earle.

these guns, rigged on standards with a long arm, were loaned from family to family when sausages were made. Such borrowing and lending was quite the custom in those days, and was considered the proper thing to do, though it was contrary to Shakespeare's advice:

Neither a borrower nor a lender be;
For borrowing loses both itself and friend,
And lending dulls the edge of husbundry.

And at slaughtering time the families were generous with their meat and shared it with neighbors, each family in turn sharing with the others. The work of butchering and preparing the meat has been described earlier. The fat was used in making lard, and that around the hog's kidneys, shaped in the form of a leaf, made what was called leaf lard, the best quality. The fat was tied in a cloth bag and thoroughly boiled in kettles. Then the bag was taken out and squeezed between squeezers of wood, to extract the fat. This hardened as lard, and was stored away in crocks. What was left in the bag was called pork scraps, a dainty morsel which appeared on the tables as late as 1895, or even later in some sections. Lard squeezers are illustrated on page 103.

Hog bristles were used in brushes, the feet were pickled, as was the head, and tallow was used for candles — so that it seems literally true that everything was used but the squeal.

Sheep and cows were killed only occasionally, but when their number became greater the animals were more often used for meat. Older generations well remember the tasty head and pluck, the latter being the name given to the heart, liver and lungs.

The hides of cows and calves were used as covering for the long wooden trunks, which were made with a lock, and had a brass handle on top. The hides were tanned with the hair left on, and this made a handsome trunk. Ornamental brass tacks fastened the hides onto the trunk and were also used in a pattern to form initials. Early trunks had rounded tops, and they were lined with wallpaper of various patterns. Later years saw a lining of newspapers,

and this showed the approximate date of the making. In the stagecoach days trunks were placed under the seats, each passenger being allowed a certain amount of weight in baggage when he engaged his place.

Hides also went into clothing, for leather is warm and durable. Before domestic animals were plentiful in the new country, wild animals, including bears and deer, were killed for their hides as well as for meat. Caps, leggings, jackets and breeches were made from the leather, and it was occasionally put to use to make a sieve for the barn or pantry.

Before the days became too cold, the animals and also the poultry were driven to market. This was done by cowherds or field-drivers, and often young boys went along to learn the work. It took several days to go to market, for cattle and swine choose their own gait and the attendants had to adjust themselves to the animals' wishes. At night, a stop was made at a tavern, the cattle and swine being put up in enclosed pastures, and the keepers resting in bunks in the tavern. Lodging cost little, and was doubtless sometimes paid by livestock given in exchange. It must have been an odd sight to see the lines of cattle or swine or turkeys or geese moving along the roads day after day, until the markets, often at a great distance, were reached.

Turkeys were usually driven to market, to be sold alive. With the coming of night, the birds would take to the trees, and this would be their roosting place until the morning sun rose in the sky. They chose their own time of roosting and the keepers had to make their stop coincide, wherever it happened to be. This was another strange sight in the fall of the year — the turkeys roosting in the branches along the road, and at daybreak coming down to the road again, to be gathered into formation for another day's journey.

Charcoal-making, which came at the end of the harvest, fell to the lot of one of the men in the family. It was a common industry, for charcoal was needed by the blacksmiths and in the later years was used for stoves, which put in their appearance following the ingenious ideas of Benjamin Franklin. The powder from charcoal was used as fertilizer and in medicines.

There were two ways to lay wood when making charcoal, one being to lay the sticks two by two and thus make a chimney, while the other was to stack the sticks in wigwam formation, bringing the tops to a point. Sometimes a pit was dug to hold the foundation, but more often the stack was built on the ground. The whole was covered with sod, with an opening left where the worker might watch the smoldering wood and see that no flame burst forth. It took several days for the operation, and during all this time the charcoal maker ate his food and took short naps there alone on the hillside, keeping guard to see that the wood did not flame. When the embers fell to the ground within the frame, the sod was stripped off and the charcoal was gathered in baskets, which were large, strongly woven ones of splint, with open spaces in the bottom. The charcoal was taken up with a long-handled scoop that had a head of tin, with many holes in it, like a strainer. This allowed the powder and finer pieces to fall through. Such a charcoal scoop is shown in the illustration. The larger pieces remaining in the basket were emptied into a barrel, and the powder was put into another barrel or a tub. The two woods that produced the best charcoal were the maple and birch, and as these trees were common, charcoal-making was quite generally carried on. Both the charcoal and the powder were sold commercially.

The fall of the year was the time for gathering more than just the harvest of grain, fruits and vegetables. There were hops to pick for brewing; herbs and roots to be dried and used for medicinal purposes; spruce gum to be taken from the cracks of the spruce trees; and nuts to be gathered and stored up attic — walnuts, hickory nuts or shagbarks, chestnuts and beechnuts. These were to be cracked and eaten in front of the fire on winter nights, and they were also used in making dyes. There were leaves to be gathered for stuffing mattresses and for laying on the floor of the ovens when loaves of bread were set in to bake; and pitch-pine knots

to be hunted out and dug from the dead trees. When old trees fell to the ground, the decaying wood caused the knots to loosen, making it easier to gather them. Pine knots were also used in the tar industry, especially along the Hudson.

All of these things that the white man gathered and used he learned about from the Indians, and it was Indian lore that became the backbone of the life of the white settlers. Without that lore, life in the wilds, fighting Nature step by step, season by season, could hardly have been carried on successfully.

When winter came in the North, it brought deep snows that piled high in impassable drifts, and extreme cold, lasting the season through and causing much hardship. But the stern northern climate produced men and women who were rugged and sturdy, and who had certain characteristics brought out by the nature of the seasons.

Around the great fire where logs burned day and night, the family ate, slept, worked — near the only heat that was afforded. The men tended their livestock during the day, and evening found them sitting by the fire whittling and creating wooden tools and implements. Wooden ware of a thousand shapes took form — boxes, buckets, bowls, plates, pantry tools, spoons, small tools used in weaving, and barn tools both large and small. The young boys, too, were busy making many things. No doubt the women folk suggested needed contrivances, for it was they who worked with most of the tools, and who felt the need of new devices.

The women had the weaving to do in the winter months, and the loom was pulled out from its corner and set for work. If the looms, spinning wheels, reels and small tools could not be made at home, they were obtained from the peddler when he made his rounds. A room was often set aside to hold the loom and here the weaving was done; but when there was no heat except that from the big fireplace, the weaving was done in the kitchen.

Young girls were taught to weave, and assisted in the weaving if they were not old enough to do it by themselves. A fifteen-year-old girl

AFTER THE WOOD HAD SMOLDERED SEVERAL DAYS AND HAD BECOME CHARCOAL, IT WAS REMOVED FROM THE SOD COVERING WITH A CHARCOAL SCOOP MADE OF TIN. IT WAS THEN PLACED IN A SPLINT CHARCOAL BASKET FOR SIFTING.

hair mesh for sieves, or a fine silk mesh, the hair and silk being called bolting cloth.

Like many tasks, when they could not be done at home, weaving was sometimes given over to a professional weaver who set up his own loom at home, or traveled from house to house in the winter months. His coming was always looked forward to, for he brought with him the current news of the villages where he had been, and exchanged gossip. He was paid for his work in supplies and cloth, for money was not used in the early years. He remained several days at each house, where he had his "keep"; all told, his life was a pleasant one. The profession of weaving often passed from generation to generation in the same family.

tells in her diary of 1790 that she wove as much as five or six yards a day, and one entry reads: "I wove two yards and three quarters and three inches today and I think I did pretty well considering that it was April Fool day." By sixteen, she was not only weaving, but "I drawed the Piece into the Harness and Sley and wove a yard."

Cloth was made for coverlets, blankets and sheets, for dresses, suits for the men, and for various small articles such as aprons, towels, bed-

Sewing was another home industry, and little children began using a needle at an early age — in the author's family, patchwork was done at the age of three as a daily stint, the little child sitting on the top step of the hall stairs and moving down, a step at a time as the work progressed. The first needlework, in addition

THESE BLOCKS WERE USED TO STAMP EMBROIDERY DESIGNS IN CLOTH. BLOCK WAS DIPPED IN AN INDELIBLE POWDER AND THEN PRESSED ON MATERIAL.

ticks and pillow cases. The cloth might be all wool; it might have cotton in it; or it might be all cotton. There were many names for the different kinds of cloth, names which sound queer and old-fashioned to us today. As the cloth came off the loom, it was put away in chests until the time when it would be used to make the needed articles. Even carpets were hand-woven, and today ingrain carpeting is highly prized as an heirloom.

Besides the large loom for weaving heavy and wide material, there was a tape loom for making tape and ribbon, called a braid or garter loom; there was a loom for braiding straw for hats; and a loom for making the finely woven

to patchwork, was that of making a sampler. It was the dread of all maidens that if they did not get married they would have to become the tailoress of the family. But no girl child went without learning to sew — there were clothes to make; patchwork quilts to piece; netting, beading, embroidering, knitting and many more hand accomplishments to learn.

Quilting bees and sewing bees were happy times, and for many of the womenfolk were the only social gatherings. These bees were the favorite seat of gossip, and were the natural point from which news circulated. The quilts were works of art and the patterns were without number, each locality designing and naming its own. Many of the patterns were beautiful, and some were most intricate; fortunately there are many hundreds of the early quilts preserved today. An old colloquial term for helping out one's neighbor with her quilting, sewing or the like was "whang," signifying exchange work. The word originally meant "to beat," and perhaps came to be used because they did beat or win out when the work was carried on by many hands.

The singing school came into existence at a time when the school house was the social center of the town. The meetings were held once or twice a week, and they were not only for young people — older members of the family joined their voices to the group. Spelling bees, too, were held, sometimes combined with the singing school, or sometimes as a meeting by themselves. In the long winter months, these social gatherings offered relaxation and enjoyment.

There were a few festive occasions which were observed regularly in the various sections. Thanksgiving was a holiday, but for many years it had no particular date. The first Thanksgiving Day was a day of prayer, giving thanks for the harvest, after that first hard winter. Fifty Puritans and ninety Indians joined the feast. The next Thanksgiving came in the spring of 1623, after a drought and famine. February 22, 1630, saw the safe arrival of ships with food and friends, and a feast of thanks was made a public affair.

It was in Massachusetts that these days were celebrated, and the date continued to be shifted from one time to another, until in 1784 Congress appointed a day. After the adoption of the Constitution, Washington appointed a day in 1789; in 1815 another day was appointed by President Madison. From 1817, Thanksgiving was an annual occasion in New York; and in 1863, the president set aside the last Thursday in November as a day of thanksgiving for the entire nation.

Christmas was not celebrated in the new land for many years for pleasure; in fact, all social life and gaiety were frowned upon by the staid Puritans, and Christmas smacked of idolatry. But eventually, being a season recognized throughout the world, the day became a holiday. Other special days were lecture days, a day of reunion, training days or muster days, when there were gatherings to watch the groups of men train, Election Day and Pope's Day, which changed to the present Fourth of July. Muster gingerbread originated with the muster days; and Election Day had its election cake.

In the winter there were itinerant workers who came with their wares and broke the monotony of the long cold months. There was the cooper, who came not only to make but to mend, and who brought his own materials and tools with which to work. He often stayed for several days. Household utensils and implements of wood were ever in demand, and as they wore out or broke down, new ones were supplied by such men if the man of the family was not handy in such work. The dish turner, too, came peddling his wares of new plates, bowls, noggins and salts.

A wheelwright traveled from village to village, carrying with him spinning wheels, which he assembled upon his arrival. The cobbler came to make shoes and boots for the entire family, bringing his tools with him. The leather was furnished by the family, skins from cows and calves being used. The cobbler received his lodging and was paid in material.

The hatter brought hats for the men, or perhaps made them on his hat molds at the time

A HAT MOLD OF PLASTER OF PARIS USED BY A TRAVELING HATTER TO SUPPLY UP-TO-DATE HEADGEAR TO CUSTOMERS LIVING IN COUNTRY DISTRICTS.

of his visit. The molds were made of plaster of Paris in a shape that was the fashion of the day. The plaster of Paris was made from deposits of gypsum, which was first burned in a kiln, then ground to a powder. When the molds were made, water was added to make a consistency of thick cream. The mold was brushed with oil before the felt was placed on it, so that the felt would not stick.

The weaver came after the linen had been bleached and prepared, and the cloth was then sent to the fuller to be dressed and dyed. As the colonists became more affluent, the tailor came twice a year, in the spring and autumn, to make clothes for the men folk. Supplying boots, shoes and clothing for the family was called "whipping the cat." Milliners and manteau-makers came to fit out the women folk.

The candlemaker went his rounds to dip candles, bringing his molds but using the tallow and wax of the family. Broom-makers came too, and these men not only made brooms, but would cut down a birch sapling and teach the young boys how to make them. Last but not least was the man who came to take pictures of the family, the pictures being called daguerreotypes, from the name of the man who invented the process, Louis Daguerre, a Frenchman. This visitor, too, stayed at the house and enjoyed the hospitality offered him, and furnished his hosts with much gossip.

All through the winter, butter-making went on, and it was a job shared by all the family. The men folk milked and brought in the milk, pouring it into shallow wooden tubs called keelers, and later into pottery dishes and tin pans. As the cream rose, the children skimmed it off with small wooden skimmers and poured it into the churn. When enough had accumulated, the churning was done by mother or grandmother.

After the butter came and was taken out

This group of butter molds shows an interesting variety of design. One in back has engraved initials, the one at left front has eagle motif, and the mold at right front holds together to make a one pound block with the letter "F" stamped into it.

of the churn, it was worked in bowls or trays of wood or in large butter workers, to free it of the remaining liquid. Then it was salted and was ready for the molds and prints. These shaped the butter and gave it a design or initial for decoration. Blocks of one pound were wrapped and weighed on wooden scales, which consisted of square wooden plates hung by cords and balanced on an arm, either suspended from the ceiling or made on a standard. No weights were used, for after the first pound of butter was made with a pound-size mold, that was used in one plate of the scale as a weight to measure the others by. Few of these old wooden butter scales have survived.

Butter was packed in tubs called firkins, or sometimes in boxes. Butter testers were used to test the purity or freshness of the butter. These were of wood or iron, and a few have been found of silver. They were long slender scoops with a short handle, which were thrust into the tub and turned around, bringing out a sample of the butter.

Each family had its own stamp on the butter; it might be an acorn, a sheaf of wheat, an eagle, a cow, flowers or initials. No other family could use the same pattern; in that way, the

In the early days, children who were unruly at church were occasionally disciplined with this kind of leather-thonged stick.

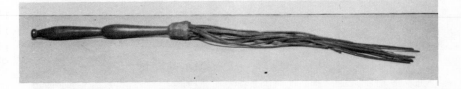

butter could be purchased with the assurance that it came from a certain family, and was of the best quality.

Going to market in wintertime with goods to sell was an occasion that was looked forward to with anticipation. In the early days, the trip was made on horseback by man and wife, carrying sacks and bundles; but when sleighs appeared, and the paths widened to passable roads, the trip became a family affair. The list of things taken was long — frozen hogs, poultry, venison, firkins of butter and cakes of cheese, bags of dried beans and peas, sheep pelts, deer hides, skins of mink, fox, fishcat and bear, besides nuts, shoepegs, yarn, stockings, mittens, homespun cloth and splint brooms. Children contributed their share of these and were allowed some of the returns.

Food was taken along for the journey, and consisted of doughnuts, sausages, roast pork, "rye and Injun" bread, cheese and frozen porridge. This last was a mess of New England beans and was considered more tasty when cold or frozen. A chunk was hung at the side of the sleigh and when anyone was hungry, he could chop off a piece and eat it. The meal on the journey was called "mitchin" or "tuck-a-nuck," old words coined by the settlers and not found in dictionaries. The family made a stop at some tavern to sleep and to have cider, hot flip or hot toddy, to refresh themselves for the long trip.

Often fifty or sixty neighbors went together in their own sleighs, either one-horse pungs or those with two horses. A sleigh might carry as much as fifty dollars' worth of goods to exchange. Coming back, the sleighs were filled with spices, raisins, fishhooks, pewter plates, English crockery, calico gowns, shawls, scarfs, hats of beaver for the men and bonnets for the women. Going to market was one of the keenest pleasures of the winter, bartering the things that had taken months to get ready and getting in return the greatest variety of things for the home or the family.

Such events, that were an integral part of existence, were important incidents in the lives of the early settlers. But it was not an existence marked by peace and serenity, as pictured so often. Life was difficult and exacting in the extreme, and each of the four seasons demanded ruggedness and hardiness and strength of character. Our forebears in those early days conquered a vast wilderness against many odds; they met hardships daily; and made the most of simple pleasures. The more we of today know about the lives they led, the more we must honor them.

THE FABULOUS DIVERSITY OF MERCHANDISE SOLD AT COUNTRY STORES OF A HUNDRED YEARS AGO IS RECREATED IN THIS FASCINATING COLLECTION OWNED BY THE LATE LAWRENCE JOHNSON OF SYRACUSE, N. Y.

Index